UPON THIS ROCK

THE CHURCH, WORK, MONEY AND YOU

Commentary by Tim Unsworth
With Activities by Jean Unsworth

ACTA Publications
Chicago, Illinois

UPON THIS ROCK
THE CHURCH, WORK, MONEY AND YOU

Commentary by Tim Unsworth
With Activities by Jean Unsworth

Editing by Rita Benz, BVM, and Gregory F. Augustine Pierce
Design by John Dylong
Typesetting by Pam Frye Typesetting

Versions of these essays appeared originally in *Salt* magazine,
205 W. Monroe, Chicago, IL 60606. Used with permission.

Scripture quotes are taken from *The New American Bible With Revised New Testament* copyright © 1986 by the Confraternity of
Christian Doctrine, Washington, D.C.

Copyright © 1991 by ACTA Publications
4848 N. Clark Street
Chicago, IL 60640
312–271–1030

Printed in the United States of America

Printing: 6 5 4 3 2 1

Year: 1996 95 94 93 92 91

Library of Congress Catalog Card Number: 91-073236

ISBN: 0–87946–059–8

DEDICATION

To three priests of the Archdiocese of Chicago who for over fifty years each have taken the church's teachings on work and economics off the printed page and brought them to life in the workaday world of the laity:

- Msgr. Daniel M. Cantwell
- Msgr. John J. Egan
- Msgr. George G. Higgins

CONTENTS

INTRODUCTION

Just west of Chicago's luxurious Gold Coast is the Cabrini–Green public housing project, one of the worst storehouses of humanity in the United States.

Cabrini–Green is filthy, crime–ridden, and devoid of stores, banks, restaurants, beauty parlors, or shoe repair shops. It is a dumping ground for the aged poor, unmarried mothers, undernourished children and other victims of virtually every social ill in American society.

It is a terrible irony that these high rise disasters bear the names of America's first saint, Mother Francis Xavier Cabrini, a naturalized U.S. citizen who dedicated her life to the poor, and William Green, one of the founders of what is today the American Federation of Labor and Congress of Industrial Organizations (AFL–CIO).

Cabrini–Green is vivid testimony to the continued need for voices and actions like those of Mother Cabrini and William Green to persuade society that our system of work and money does not serve everyone and must constantly be compelled to be more faithful to the teachings of the Bible and the church. (Green, a non–Catholic, was reported to have carried Pope Leo XIII's encyclical *Rerum Novarum* in his coat pocket.)

Over the centuries, Catholic social thought on work and money has taken many paths — some of them fruitful, some of them dead ends. For many centuries, for example, the teachings of Saint Thomas Aquinas (1225–1274) shaped the church's approach to social questions. His teaching promoted a highly structured social sphere full of duties and responsibilities but with little room for individual and group rights.

According to Aquinas, the obligation to the larger society held clear priority over personal desires and needs. Christians were expected to accept as God's will their role in life. Both civil and church leaders were to be respected and obeyed as if their words were coming directly from God. As long as people fulfilled their proper roles, tranquility would be assured. Those in charge would be moral, highly motivated individuals, willing to share their abundance with the worker who made their good fortune possible. (In a vastly oversimplified way, Aquinas's scholastic reasoning has been translated into "trickle–down," supply–side economics.)

The medieval system of which Thomas Aquinas was part died slowly. It was not until 1891 and the issuance of the encyclical *Rerum Novarum* that the church set in motion new patterns of thought on work and economics that have taken root over the years. In the past century, Catholic social teaching has had an enormous impact on social policy affecting the welfare of the worker. No longer does the church take the position that there's a place for everyone and everyone should take his or her place. Rights and responsibilities are no longer a one way street with the powerful exercising all the rights and the powerless having all the responsibilities. Now the church teaches that the state and the wealthy have obligations and that individuals and groups can act on social issues affecting their human dignity.

In 1991, the one hundredth anniversary of *Rerum Novarum*, for example, Pope John Paul II's encyclical *Centesimus Annus* draws explicit connections from the guidelines of Leo XIII to such specific issues as Social Security, unemployment benefits, injury compensation, and health insurance. These papal pronouncements have had a profound impact in the United States, where since 1919 the bishops have been issuing statements on the social order, including pastoral letters on race relations, poverty, unemployment, economic justice, and the dignity of the individual.

The anniversary of *Rerum Novarum*, therefore, is an appropriate time to revisit and reevaluate church teachings and practices on the issues of work and money as they affect us today. These essays are not intended to be in–depth studies but rather theological and historical overviews. They attempt to paint a verbal mural of the highlights and shadows of history. The questions for individual reflection and group discussion and the activities for further investigation offered at the end of each chapter are an attempt to apply the lessons of history to today's social climate and the reader's personal experience.

Jean and Tim Unsworth
Chicago, Illinois
1991 – Centenary of Rerum Novarum

1

FEUDALISM

It's been some five hundred years since the close of the chapter of European history known as the Middle Ages. But evidence from this period survives today in many ways, both subtle and obvious.

In her essay on the rise of feudalism, historian Anne Fremantle reminds readers that "the European of today may pay taxes in the same town halls; vote in the same parliament buildings; buy and sell in the same marketplaces; change his money in the same streets; roam the same castles; study within the same college walls; listen to the same bells; and worship in the same cathedrals." Relics of feudalism form the stage on which much of Europe's successful tourist business is acted out.

In this country, too, the legacy of feudalism is still with us. Economically, the feudal system has roots everywhere — in the small southern city, the Pennsylvania coal town, the small steel mill. Politically, it can be found in Chicago's ward system, in New York City's boroughs, and in company towns everywhere.

Our judgment of the feudal period as a whole must be relative. It was an age of faith, but one filled with superstition. It passed on theological treasures and pious trash. It was an age of needless pain and death. Many children were born, took one look at the world, and promptly died. On the other hand, the period marked the beginnings of advances in medical science that finally began to flourish in the post–Sputnik era.

Life was short, dangerous, and doomed. One shudders at the tortures, judicial mutilations, blindings, and beheadings of the feudal period. Yet our own impersonal mass cruelties — "surgical" bombings, Agent Orange, the use of starvation as a weapon — make feudal cruelty seem mild by comparison.

HISTORICAL ROOTS

Feudal estates first appeared in the Frankish lands during the eighth and ninth centuries. Scholars are not agreed whether the basis was Roman or German, but it can safely be said that feudalism emerged from the disintegration of Roman institutions and from the inroads of German settlements. There are traces of feudalism in the practice of the Roman landowner gradually transferring privileges to his protectors — a system that gave way to the manor structure.

Feudalism spread from France to Spain and then to Italy and Eastern Europe. Gradually, as the lord extended his power, the manor house was replaced by the feudal castle with its town and surrounding farms. In England, feudalism arrived with William the Conqueror in 1066, although certain aspects of it appeared before that.

THE CHURCH AND FEUDALISM

There was only one church in feudal times. If one was not baptized in it, one was not considered a member of society. If one was excommunicated by the church, he or she lost all political and legal rights as well. Women were barely considered in this equation. Typically, Saint Boniface in the early eighth century forbade women to go on pilgrimages, observing that "for the most part, they are lost, few remaining pure."

The church had a great influence in shaping feudalism. Although the church itself did not become feudal in character, its hierarchy paralleled the feudal structure. The church held much land, largely through its monasteries, its dignitaries, and its churches. In time, the church's holdings took on a feudal look, with the bishop or abbot ruling like a lord.

Medieval Christians were required to tithe—donate a full ten percent of their incomes—to the church, with one-quarter of the tithe going to the bishop, the poor, the clergy, and the parish, respectively. The peasants often wished that there were not so many intermediaries between themselves and their religious responsibilities. There was a measure of anticlericalism, a syndrome that would become more common over the years.

At the same time, this was also the church that provided sanctuary for the endangered folks who took refuge within its walls. It was the church that insisted that the poor did not have to fast as much as the rich. It was the church that provided the poor with social services—including free food and free hospitalization. For a long time, the church was the only source of education. Through its schools, the church passed on what was left of the classical past, especially the unifying Latin language.

It was a period of great devotion. Saints' days were marked on the calendar with red letters (hence our "red-letter" days). Miracles were everywhere; relics abounded. One could touch the sponge offered to Christ on the cross or view his swaddling clothes. Saint Thomas Aquinas, who fell ill and died in the monastery of Fossa Nuova, Italy, was decapitated and his body boiled to preserve his bones for relics!

Not many feudal lords functioned without a prelate at their sides. "The seamless garment of Christ" referred to a unity of beliefs that was fiercely protected. (It would emerge in the 1980s with a different meaning, a concept of respect for all life.) Little wonder the feudal period has been called "the age of faith."

Many of the current beliefs and practices of Catholics were established during the feudal period. Transubstantiation was made a dogma in 1215; the number of sacraments was fixed at seven. The doctrine of "the treasury of the merits of the church" was proposed in the thirteenth century and confirmed soon after. This doctrine held that through prayer, good deeds, pilgrimages, and even cash contributions believers could obtain an "indulgence" or a draft on the treasury that contained the excess virtues of Christ and the saints. The treasury was to be drawn upon by the performers of these good works to relieve themselves or others of purgatorial pains.

CREATIVITY, STABILITY AND GENEROSITY

There was much to admire in feudal society. It was fixed and stable, and within it most people could find contentment. They knew the rules; they were not assailed by futile questionings and anxieties. There's a good chance that their mental health was better than ours.

The period accomplished great things in architecture and the arts, in literature and learning. It added grace, beauty, and comfort to living. The larger feudal estates — forerunners of our cities — produced Dante, Boccaccio, Giotto, and Fra Angelico.

Feudal society initiated industrialist and capitalist concepts that unleashed incredible forces, both good and bad. There was much of socialism in the guilds and communism in the monasteries. Feudal times developed the spirit of discovery that was to expand humanity's geographical, spiritual, and material universe.

For the people of feudal society, life was secure. People had a closeness to God and the saints. The saints hovered just a few yards overhead, ready with miracles and answers to prayers, most of which had to do with another's welfare. Almsgiving was one of the best observed tenets of people's religion. There was even a special dish at the table where people placed a portion of their food for the poor. Beggars were outside every church; mendicant monks with their begging bowls were everywhere. People gave a more generous portion of their income than they do today.

A TIME OF SOCIAL PROGRESS

To this day, some scholars view feudalism as a necessary stage in political development. It represented sanity after centuries of barbarian hordes. The Middle Ages trained physicians and lawyers; craftsmen made reading glasses for scholars so that they could read in their old age; slavery, which the ancients and even early church people had thought to be inevitable, almost entirely disappeared. Serfdom was gradually abolished in some regions and mitigated in others. Free people began toying with representative government and eventually learned to talk back to kings.

There was much more. Trial by jury, the rise of middle–class society, universities, banks, innovative farming methods, the development of Europe's famous vineyards, the introduction of literacy, the evolution of the *scriptorium* where monks inscribed precious books, guilds — these developments all had their beginnings during this era, which is so often misconstrued as simply bleak and barren, a mere prelude to the Renaissance.

CLASS AND AUTHORITY

In an era of almost no political unity, central authority within a given country was almost unknown. The only common bond was people's Christian faith, to which their links were both politically and spiritually strong.

There was a strict division into social classes: nobility, clergy, peasantry and — late in the period — a middle class. Feudal castles were governed by local custom, and there was a landholding system that was based on a fee (the fief). The ideal feudal society held that ownership of all land be ultimately vested in the king, but that ideal of unity and authority was really a legal fiction. In fact, each fiefdom was a mini–kingdom, with each local lord a sovereign over his vassals.

Beneath the king existed a hierarchy of nobles. The most important nobles held land directly from the king; less influential persons received their land from the nobles, and so forth, until one got down to the *seignior*, who owned only a manor. The manor itself was a self–contained enterprise with a separate hierarchy, with the *seignior* granting the use of land to serfs in return for personal services or dues. Sometimes, these serfs would create subfiefdoms, granting part of their land to a lesser vassal.

For the most part serfs, called *villeins* (from *villa*, meaning "farm"), were given the use of more than forty acres as well as the right to draw water from the lord's springs and gather wood from his forests. In exchange, serfs had to labor for a prescribed number of days and supply the lord with produce from their own farms. At the bottom of the social and economic pile were the *cotters* (hence "cottage"), who were given perhaps three or four acres to farm but who also had to serve as menials in the manor house.

Few serfs questioned their status. It was their duty to support the nobles and the clergy. In return, they understood that the church would supply their spiritual needs and that the nobles would govern fairly and provide security. Noblemen had their obligations to the serfs, hence the phrase *noblesse oblige* (literally "nobility obliges"). Initially, money played only a small part in the feudal system. Bartering of products and services was common. Written contracts were almost unknown until later; the handshake or the kiss sealed the deal. The lord also offered a forum to settle property disputes among his vassals.

It was possible for peasants to work their way up the ladder. Legally, at least, they were free to move from their farms and into the feudal town. They could purchase freedom in exchange for a year's labor and then learn a skill in one of the craft guilds. In the early estates, the lords themselves were barely out of the peasant class, although later there was a very strict system of class, status and inheritance by birth. Church people advanced in the hierarchy, although most of the higher clergy came from high–ranking families.

In some ways feudalism was a good system. At least it was a vast improvement over the mess society had become after the fall of the Roman Empire. (Thomas Aquinas thought feudalism to be the ideal societal structure.)

NEGATIVE ASPECTS

In modern parlance, however, the feudal system could be termed labor intensive. It was an economy dependent almost entirely on agriculture and on a peasant class that would permanently consist of about ninety percent of the population.

A manor of some three thousand acres might have only a dozen families to do all the fieldwork, ditch–digging, road–mending, and manure–carrying. In addition, serfs were often expected to do boon work — extra service as a sign of gratitude for the lord's protection. The lord could impose extra taxes: a head tax, income tax, or payments for the use of the lord's oven, mill, or wine press. Sometimes a serf had to pay for the right to marry a woman from another manor.

The goal of the manor was self–sufficiency, much like the plantations and farms of early America. Often this ideal was not reached. Though a manor could feed, clothe, and house its inhabitants, it had to import such things as salt for curing meat and iron for its blacksmith. The manor had to pay for these materials out of farm surpluses. A bad crop could upset the delicate economic balance.

The lack of political unity among the estates led to some fighting, and soon the lords needed armed warriors for protection. As conflicts increased, the nobility became essentially a military class with the picturesque knight as the typical warrior. In time, the lords required each vassal to supply soldiers for their armies.

Putting a knight on a horse was an expensive project. The lord had to reward his noblemen in order to ensure their loyalty and their financial support. Thus came the origins of counts, dukes, and barons — even the lowly squire, who ranked below the knight.

Remnants of this nobility system exist today. They are most visible in modern England, where Queen Elizabeth's children still enjoy income from their fiefdoms and where knighthood is extended for extraordinary service. Under different names, traces of feudalism are also evident in the American political "spoils," or "patronage," system. The church, too, still has its various groupings of knights and monsignors.

JUSTICE

Lords frequently offered their vassals a role in the justice system in return for financial support. These vassals often sat in as associate justices in disputes involving property and conduct. Rich or noble defendants could bring in their "oath helpers," whose job was to verify the testimony of their masters (even if it were false). The facts of a case were often far less important to the judges than the reliability or reputations of the defendants.

Justice in feudal times was often primitive, coarse, and cruel. Every castle had its dungeon, but few criminals spent much time in confinement. More often they were beaten, branded, or mutilated; their eyes gouged out or their hands cut off. Torture was habitual and often administered under the eyes of the lord. If a court was confused about guilt, it resorted to a trial by ordeal to find who was telling the truth. The accused could be told to carry a red–hot iron for nine feet. If the wound healed within three days, his or her veracity was established. If not, the burned hand was the least of the person's troubles.

Sometimes, two claimants would be required to engage in "judicial combat" — a figure of speech today but a reality then. They fought with wooden shields and sharp picks until one yielded. The loser was judged guilty and generally hanged immediately.

Swift justice kept believers in line. Under Charlemagne (742–814) — who might be called the "father of feudalism" and who appointed bishops and supervised lower clergy — the death penalty was imposed for such religious offenses as breaking a Lenten fast or eating meat on Friday. Thus did church and civil disciplines merge.

TOWNS AND GUILDS

Gradually, Europe began to take on the look associated with the word medieval. Towns and monasteries sprouted thick new walls; fortified castles were built. (Before quarries could provide large amounts of stone, early castles were built of wood, not unlike the log forts of the American frontier.) By the twelfth century, castles had become enormous places with turrets, complicated passageways, workshops, stalls, etc. Animals wandered everywhere; sanitation was virtually nonexistent; the castle was far noisier (and smellier) than a modern city street.

Medieval people were the ultimate small–towners; the lower classes would spend entire lifetimes within only two square miles. The feudal town was closely linked to the surrounding countryside. It produced largely for the local market. Peasants were required by law to sell to the nearest town — a rule that assured the community its food supply and kept down speculation.

On Saturday, the local artisans had to close their shops and exhibit their wares in an official marketplace (the first shopping malls?), thus giving the buyers a chance to compare prices. The powerful guilds were associations of merchants, craftsmen, or provisioners. Butchers, bakers, goldsmiths, tanners, carpenters, and cloth merchants banded together; each group made rules governing its own trade.

They were less interested in consumer protection than in preventing cutthroat competition, oversupply, and economic chaos. The apprentice system instituted by these guilds served as an important education component, one that survives today in the modern skilled–worker or craft unions.

The guilds also exercised considerable political power. Guildsmen stood high in the town's social hierarchy. Guilds had their banners, their patron saints, their processions, and their feast days. They took an active part in the embellishment of the local church, providing funds for this or that window or chapel. With the breakup of the feudal system, the church lost much of that link with the working class. It is a breakup from which neither side has ever fully recovered.

THE END OF FEUDALISM

The feudal system flourished until the fourteenth century, when it began to fade. The greatest disruptive force was within the system itself, namely, too much power in the hands of a few. The rise of powerful monarchs in France, Spain, and England weakened the local system. Another disruptive force was the increase of commerce and communication that broke down the isolation of the manor, assisted in the rise of the towns, and facilitated the emergence of the middle class. The system changed gradually. It was not completely destroyed in France until the French Revolution (1789). It persisted in Germany until 1848 and in Russia and Ireland until 1917.

In retrospect, feudal society was not the best possible, but it was a vast improvement over the previous system. Ultimately, feudal society formed the basis of the Western civilization that we know today.

QUESTIONS FOR REFLECTION
AND GROUP DISCUSSION

1. The sense of community in a contained society such as a feudal estate had some advantages and some disadvantages. Compare feudal society to society today in terms of care for those in need, communal celebrations, unity of faith, work, family life and other issues.

2. The *noblesse oblige* of the noble class was a measure of their obligation to those under them and was regulated only by their personal generosity. How does that attitude compare with the concept of paternalism? What about the idea of stewardship?

3. The emergence of the guilds and the recognition they gave to a worker's mastery of skills and quality of work was a large step out of feudalism and into the humanism of the Renaissance. Is there a comparable system today to develop an individual's skills? Do unions offer this kind of education and status? What more could be done by church and society to recognize the work of the individual skilled worker?

4. How do aspects of the feudal system continue today in church or society? Explain how you feel they are useful or harmful.

5. Women in the age of chivalry seemed idealized, but Saint Boniface's observation that they were "for the most part lost, few remaining pure" suggests an entirely different attitude. In what ways does Boniface's view of women still persist in the church and society?

ACTIVITIES FOR FURTHER INVESTIGATION

1. Imagine yourself as a member of a feudal society. Divide your group into nobility (lords and ladies, knights, squires), clergy (bishops, priests, monks), peasantry (vassals, cotters, serfs) and plot out a day's activities for each group. Confront a problem of injustice together. Plan and carry out a liturgical celebration.

2. View the videotape of *The Return of Martin Guerre*. Discuss what you felt and learned from the movie.

3. It was during the feudal age that Gregorian plainchant was composed and sung. Try singing plainchant at a liturgy.

4. In the pre–printing press era, the Middle Ages produced the treasures of manuscripts lettered and decorated by monks. Find and enjoy examples in your library.

5. It was from feudal manors that the Crusaders were drawn. Read about their origins, goals, and pursuits.

USURY

In a society like ours in which one can borrow money for an indefinite period of time to meet the price of an already–consumed restaurant meal (albeit often at rates of more than twenty percent annually), usury must seem like an inconsequential vice, as dated as the sinfulness of eating meat on Friday.

Usury (lending money at exorbitant or illegal rates) demands our attention today, however, because it contains trace elements of the social, economic, and moral disaster found in many parts of the world. Observe the present plight of nations such as Brazil, Mexico, and Argentina, for example, which cannot meet legally established interest payments on loans from U.S. banks. Or estimate the number of foreclosures on homes and farms in this country in which families cannot repay mortgages at even relatively modest interest rates of ten or twelve percent. As for other forms of credit, if an economic crisis caused all creditors to call in their loans immediately and at the same time, some experts hold that the U.S. would experience a depression that would make the crash of 1929 appear to be a mere glitch on the historical financial charts.

While usury remains an important social issue, respected scholars such as John T. Noonan ruefully conclude that it is a "dead issue today" and "is not likely to stir to life." In Noonan's view, however, the study of usury reveals a great deal about the relations between religion, reason, and economic facts, especially in the Western world.

HISTORICAL PERSPECTIVES

The ethics of charging interest is one of civilization's oldest disputes. In ancient times, usury referred to the charging of any interest on almost any loan, especially loans on perishable goods. (The word derives from the Latin word *usura*, meaning "a charge.")

Modest interest on loans had been collected since the beginning of historical records, but greed eventually changed its purpose and complexion. Interest rates became exorbitant and penalties for late payment heavy. Eventually, the practice of usury fell into disrepute and has been scorned ever since.

Greek law did not forbid the taking of interest, but it did regulate it. Plato (427?–347? B.C.) condemned usury as inimical to the welfare of the state because it set one class—poor borrowers—against another class—wealthy lenders. Aristotle (384–322 B.C.) wrote in *Politics* that the most hated sort of money–making was usury: "Money was intended to be used in exchange but not to increase at interest. Of all modes of getting wealth, this is the most unnatural."

Aristotle considered the usurer guilty of injustice, pettiness, and illiberality. He held that interest by its very nature violates justice. He declared money to be a "barren (or sterile) thing, incapable of reproduction." Hence, interest in effecting the "birth of money from money" was considered contrary to nature and a violation of justice. The philosopher held that justice required that a borrower return only an equal sum to a lender, with no interest at all.

Roman law defined interest as a right to compensation for a loss suffered by the lender when the borrower failed to return a loan on time, a concept of usury that survived until the Middle Ages. But usury was no more popular among the Romans than it was among the Greeks, although Roman law was a little more liberal than the Greek statutes. (Roman law set maximum legal interest rates at twelve percent, a practice that remained in effect until the Code of Justinian (A.D. 529) permitted varying interest rates that were pegged to the status of the borrower.)

BIBLICAL PERSPECTIVES

The Old Testament forbids the charging of *any* interest on loans to the poor or to other Jews: "If you lend money to one of your poor neighbors among my people, you shall not act like an extortioner toward him by demanding interest from him" (Ex 22:24). "If one of your kinsmen in any community is in need in the land which the Lord, your God, is giving to you, you shall not harden your heart nor close your hand to him in his need. Instead, you shall open your hand to him and freely lend him enough to meet his need" (Dt 15:7–8). "You shall not demand interest from your countrymen on a loan of money or of food or of anything else on which interest is usually demanded" (Dt 23:20).

The Psalmist sings that the person who dwells in the Lord's presence is one "who lends not his money at usury" (Ps 15:5). Ezekiel puts the moneylender in the same category as one who looks at idols or defiles his neighbor's wife (Ez 18:10–13). Nehemiah (5:10) virtually shouts, "Let us put an end to this usury!" when he learns that the Jewish people were being forced to mortgage their fields, vineyards, and homes to get grain. Some were even mortgaging their children into slavery. Job (24:3) bemoans the fact that usurers "take the widow's ox for a pledge."

The New Testament makes no direct reference to the ethics of interest, but there are inferences. Paul terms love of money "the root of all evils" (1 Tim 6:10). The parable of the talents would appear to praise the practice of increasing one's wealth by charging interest, but that may be stretching Jesus's point. In the Sermon on the Mount (Lk 6:34–35), for example, Jesus takes the Old Testament tradition a step further. Gospel love directs that a loan should be an outright gift. "If you lend money to those from whom you expect repayment," he says "what credit is that to you? Even sinners lend to sinners, and get back the same amount. But rather, love your enemies and do good to them, and lend expecting nothing back. . . ."

THE CHURCH AND USURY

It is clear that pagans, Jews, and early Christians alike all detested the practice of charging interest of any kind, especially on loans to the poor. Such attitudes affected church teaching for many centuries.

The immorality of usury still remains part of the church's teaching, although the church's teaching on usury — as well as on such topics as religious liberty and the role of sex in marriage — has inarguably changed over the centuries. Some scholars believe that such experience with change could allow the church to alter its present teaching on such other issues as contraception, divorce and remarriage, celibacy, and the ordination of women.

Early church fathers merely repeated the scriptural teachings, stating that exacting usury of the poor is contrary to charity and mercy. The Council of Arles (A.D. 314) forbade the practice of usury to all clerics; and in A.D. 345 the Council of Carthage declared the practice of usury as reprehensible for laypeople. The Council of Nicea (A.D. 325) was particularly harsh on clerics who got involved in the loan business. "Since many clerics, filled with avarice and with the spirit of usury," the Council said, "forget the sacred words and demand usuriously (that is every month a rate of interest), the great and holy synod declares that if anyone, after publication of this law, takes interest, no matter on what grounds, or carries on the business of usurer, no matter in what ways. . . he must be turned out of the clergy and his name struck off the list."

Later church councils repeated these sentiments. The great councils of the Middle Ages — Lateran III (1179), Lyons II (1247), and Vienne (1311) — all condemned usury. The Council of Vienne claimed that anyone who did not believe that usury was sinful was a heretic. For medieval theologians such as Thomas Aquinas, the evil of usury lay not only in its origins but also in its effects. The greed of the lenders resulted in exploitation and oppression, driving the poor to despair, slavery, even suicide.

This was tough teaching by the church, but not if one likens usury to present loan–sharking practices in poor neighborhoods, where interest compounded daily can reach annual rates as high as fifty percent. Before drug–pushing became its primary source of income, organized crime syndicates made a substantial portion of their income from these high–interest loans, and it's still a major part of that business.

Such strong church condemnation of usury probably also applies to situations like those in which shrewd tax lawyers take property from old and sometimes senile people by simply satisfying an unpaid tax claim for them and then stealing their property. Usurious practices of the kind condemned by the early church are still common in many Third World countries.

CONFUSION ON THE ISSUE

Despite its long opposition to usury, however, no-where in council documents or scholastic teaching is it stated definitively that the charging of interest in itself and under all circumstances is a violation of justice. In fact, Aquinas taught that any loss sustained or any profit forgone by the lender as a result of a loan could permit some additional repayment. Still, any hint of usury was clearly condemned and even the charging of interest was viewed with the greatest suspicion throughout Christendom.

(Muslim countries, long active in trade, found ways to circumvent the prohibition of usury in their holy book, *The Qur'an (Koran)*. They often charged a higher purchase price when payment was deferred. Jews also engaged in moneylending at interest, leading to Shakespeare's creation of the stereotyped Jewish usurer Shylock in *The Merchant of Venice*.)

With the expansion of trade throughout Europe beginning in the thirteenth century, the demand for credit — and interest paid on that credit — increased, necessitating a modification of the popular concept of usury. Gradually, the word usury came to mean the charging of exorbitant or unconscionable interest rates. Simply stated, low rates became known as interest; high rates were called usury. By the close of the Middle Ages, the use of interest had expanded a great deal, some secular legislation was falling into place. By 1545, England, for example, had fixed a legal maximum amount of interest, a practice that was followed by most Western countries. (Today, Great Britain does not fix interest rates, but courts determine whether or not a rate is usurious.)

By the sixteenth century, church teaching on usury began to change somewhat because economic conditions had changed. According to theologian Father Richard P. McBrien, changing factors "made the old condemnation obsolete." The experiences of lay Christians had to be heeded. Thus, he cites Navarrus (1586), a professor at Salamanca and the author of *A Manual for Confessors*, in which Navarrus argues that "an infinite number of decent Christians" were engaged in banking. He objected to any analysis that would "damn the whole world."

Three papal statements over a seventeen year period (1569-1586) unequivocally denounced usury, but their impact died almost in the telling. Christian laity continued to charge and pay interest as if the prohibitions did not exist. Gradually, instead of being seen as "sterile," money was seen as productive. Furthermore, interest charges served to equalize the value of present and future amounts of money.

The church tried to keep pace with changing economic conditions. In 1745, Benedict XIV issued an encyclical, *Vix Pervenit*, in which he tried to clear up some questions about the church's position on usury. The confusion among the faithful on the issue, however, continued. In the nineteenth century, the Vatican issued fourteen different statements that concluded that Christians who lend money at moderate rates "are not to be disturbed." In 1891, however, Leo XIII in his monumental encyclical, *Rerum Novarum*, again cried out against what he termed a "devouring usury" that "although often condemned by the church, but practiced nevertheless under another form by avaricious and grasping men, had increased the evil [of economic injustice]."

MODERN PERSPECTIVES

The moral and ethical chess match over the morality of charging and paying interest continued into modern times.

Scottish political economist Adam Smith (1723–1790) in his book *The Wealth of Nations* concluded that all the regulations against usury only served to increase the evil of it. He suggested that people should pay for the use of money as they do for everything else.

Smith had a point. As with our current tax laws, as quickly as the prohibitions on usury were announced, some creative loophole was devised. Compound interest replaced simple interest. Points paid on mortgages are nothing more than interest paid in advance, permitting lending institutions to charge more interest than the law might allow. Bonuses, commissions, and fees are just a few of the other ways in which lenders can garner additional interest above the so–called "market rate."

Today, the church's attitude toward interest has changed considerably. Lending money at a fair rate of interest is now seen as an acceptable and even positive endeavor. The Vatican itself now lends money at interest. Local dioceses and churches do the same. Socially committed religious and secular institutions attempt to relieve certain social stresses by actually lending money at low rates of interest to needy individuals and groups. Government at every level assists poor people with low–interest housing and educational loans.

Long–term, low–interest loans to needy countries can allow them to learn to make the proverbial "loaf of bread" for themselves rather than have to rely on handouts that are often marked with political price tags. On the other hand, church teaching on usury might help address the problem of the billions of dollars in loans that have already been amassed by needy countries. Pedro Casaldalgia, CMF, Bishop of Mato Grosso, Brazil, has said that it would be a "sin" for

First World banks to collect the over one hundred billion dollar debt owed by his country. He told *Maryknoll* magazine "The debt has already been collected. It was collected by taking our natural resources and our super–cheap labor. It was collected in our infant mortality and in the blood, the deaths of our people." A revisiting of the biblical and church prohibition on usury might lead governments and people to understand the need and the rationale for forgiving all or part of that debt.

QUESTIONS FOR REFLECTION
OR GROUP DISCUSSION

1. Do you agree with the biblical and early church abhorrence of charging any form of interest on money lent — especially to poor people? Explain your response.

2. What are some of the positive aspects of moneylending and borrowing for the ordinary person today? Consider specifics of home mortgages, IRAs, pension funds, insurance, stock ownership, and banking interest.

3. Usury as exorbitant interest can be seen today in credit cards. Discuss and compute the hidden costs of credit card debt and the "buy now, pay later" attitude it encourages.

4. Shylock in *The Merchant of Venice* required a pound of flesh if a debt was not repaid on time. Evaluate this as a metaphor for the price people pay today for borrowing. Do you feel that foreclosure and bankruptcy are appropriate penalties for accumulating too much debt? Why or why not?

5. What do you think of Bishop Casaldalgia's position on the Third World debts to First World banks: "The debt has already been collected by taking our natural resources and our super–cheap labor. It was collected in our infant mortality and in the blood, the deaths of our people."

ACTIVITIES FOR FURTHER INVESTIGATION

1. Add together all the interest your family paid out in the past two years — including mortgage payments. Check the current national debt and what steps are being taken to alleviate it. Discover what percentage of the current federal budget goes to pay interest on past debts. Ask about the total debt of your parish and diocese.

2. As a group, pool money to buy one share of a stock. Watch its progress for a month or a year. Compare the increase in price and the dividends you receive from the stock to the interest you would have earned by putting the money in an insured certificate of deposit. Was the additional risk of buying the stock worth the difference?

3. Do a dramatic reading of *The Merchant of Venice* by William Shakespeare. Memorize Portia's speech that begins "The quality of mercy is not strained. . ."

4. Gather ads for credit cards and evaluate the sales tactics used and the possible consequences to card users.

5. List and compare ways open to the ordinary person to derive income from investments. Compare get–rich–quick investments with socially responsible investments.

3
CAPITALISM

In the closing months of 1988, Kohlberg Kravis Roberts & Co., a powerful leveraged buyout firm, negotiated a twenty-five billion dollar purchase of RJR Nabisco Inc. (This amount was more than the gross national product (GNP) of Portugal that year.) Even in the jaded world of professional business watchers, the sale was described variously as "titanic," "obsessive," and "obscene." For some, the Nabisco buyout was the epitome of capitalist success. For others, it symbolized everything that is wrong with the capitalist system.

The ripple effect of the deal touched virtually every American. The buyout put the company in enormous debt; the jobs of many of Nabisco's one hundred and twenty thousand employees were threatened; the federal government lost an estimated one billion dollars in tax revenues; the prices of the company's goods rose. Who actually benefited from this deal? A handful of business executives, brokers, and lawyers enriched themselves enormously.

This example does not mean that capitalism is necessarily an economic system based on greed and selfishness. It is capable of operating justly within the humane community. The recent collapse of communism in eastern Europe and even the Soviet Union itself have shown the attractiveness of a free market economy. At its best, capitalism can and does—just as the U.S. Constitution envisioned—"establish justice" and "promote the general welfare." On the other hand, capitalism has shown itself to be capable of the most egregious abuses, all in the name of "freedom," "risk taking," and "competition."

THE CHURCH AND CAPITALISM

Catholic social teaching does not endorse any one economic arrangement. It sets policy. It offers guidelines. The society envisioned by Catholic social teaching is one in which private property is respected. Based on the philosophical thought of Thomas Aquinas, the Catholic Church has taught that private property enables the human development intended by the Creator. Yet, as University of Notre Dame professor Father Oliver F. Williams, CSC, points out, "The teaching has always insisted that private property has a social dimension which requires that owners consider the common good in the use of property." ("Common good" is a term used frequently in Catholic social teaching to refer to the total environment — cultural, social, religious, political, and economic — required for the living of fully human lives by all people.)

In his book *The Common Good and U.S. Capitalism*, Williams states that "the vision of society assumes some persons will have more material goods than others but that the affluent will provide for the less fortunate, either through the channels of public policy or other appropriate groups of society."

The Nabisco deal represented capitalism at its worst. Neither the natural–law perspective of Thomas Aquinas nor the faith–and–gospel approach of Vatican II teaching were considered. It would be hard to argue that the common good demanded by Catholic social teaching was served by the transaction. From that point of view, the deal was an ethical and moral disaster. Because of the buyout, for example, homemakers will pay more for basic food products so that a few rich people can add to their already great wealth. Such a result strains the boundaries of ethical capitalism.

What can be termed Christian capitalism strives to maintain a delicate balance between the free organization of capital and labor in permanent cooperation for the common good. It's a neat trick. The *New York Times* has editorialized that there can be "no facile resolution of the conflict between the values of a just society and the sharply opposing values of a successful corporation."

In his 1991 encyclical, *Centesimus Annus*, Pope John Paul II praised capitalism's potential to do good: "The free market is the most efficient instrument for utilizing resources and effectively responding to needs." On the other hand, the pope repeated centuries–old church skepticism and warnings about the problems inherent in the capitalist system. "The church has no models to present," he wrote. "The church offers her social teaching as an indispensable and ideal orientation, a teaching which recognizes the positive value of the market and of enterprise, but which at the same time points out that these need to be oriented toward the common good."

HISTORICAL PERSPECTIVES

Capitalism — also called the free–market economy or free enterprise — has been dominant in the Western world since the breakdown of feudalism. The term itself is of more recent origin. It was first used by Louis Blanc (1811–1882) in his book *Organisation du Travail (The Organization of Work)*. Karl Marx (1818–1883) didn't even use the word in his three volume work *Das Capital (Capital)*. The phrase did not come into common usage until the early 1900s. The key concept of capitalism is that most of the means of production are privately (rather than publicly) owned. Production is guided and income is distributed largely through the operation of the markets (rather than by state–run planning).

Capitalism as we know it traces to the sixteenth century, but antecedents of capitalist institutions existed in the ancient world. During the hunting and fishing stage of civilization, physical capital (weapons and tools) and financial capital (primitive money) were individually owned and used. Almost as written history began, there appeared merchants, manufacturers, and financiers — the forerunners of modern capitalists. Still, it was generally the absolute monarch in the ancient world who set overall economic policy. By the Middle Ages, however, pockets of free enterprise were flourishing in Europe.

The advent of capitalism was tied closely to the Protestant Reformation of the sixteenth century. The traditional religious disdain for acquisitive effort was diminished by the "Protestant ethic." Hard work and frugality were given stronger religious sanction. Prosperity was seen as a sign of God's approval. In time, as economic inequality resulted, it was justified on the grounds that the wealthy were also the virtuous.

Another factor contributing to capitalism was the increase in Europe's supply of precious metals, such as silver and gold. This led to an inflation of prices. W. P. Webb, in his book *The Great Frontier*, contends that modern capitalism also had its roots in the discovery and exploitation of three massive continents — North America, Asia and Africa. The pioneers in these countries were caught in a "trap of freedom," he maintains, and the enormous riches there fueled the growth of capitalism.

Early modern capitalists (1500–1750) also enjoyed the rise of bigger and stronger nation states and the introduction of uniform monetary systems and legal codes. Banks and the courts quickly became the servants of the capitalists. By the eighteenth century, capitalism began to shift its emphasis from commerce to industry. Capital invested in centralized manufacturing plants helped create the Industrial Revolution, and the invention of complex machinery only speeded the process.

IDEOLOGICAL PERSPECTIVES

In time, an ideology was developed to support what was already happening. During the eighteenth century, the doctrine of economic liberalism was developed by a group of French thinkers who believed that the natural laws that explain the phenomena of the physical world had their counterpart in economic, social, and political relationships. They believed that the activities of the state should not interfere with this order but should instead be confined to police protection and the administration of justice. The doctrine became known as *laissez–faire* from the French for "to leave alone or let be".

Scottish economist Adam Smith's *The Wealth of Nations* (1776) recommended leaving economic decisions to the free play of self–regulating market forces. Smith argued that when each person pursues his or her own self–interest, the common good is automatically enhanced. Thus, the baker bakes the best bread he can and sells it at the best price possible so that he can use the proceeds of the sale to buy those things he wants or needs, and this cycle is repeated over and over in countless individual cases.

Smith sought freedom from the religious control of business and industry that had marked the mercantile period. Prior to the existence of capitalism, religious teaching had condemned attempts by individuals to climb to a higher level of living through economic activity. Furthermore, many church practices were economically inefficient. Some towns in medieval Europe, for example, had over one hundred holy days or holidays each year.

Aristotle, Thomas Aquinas, and many of the early teachers of the church had a certain disdain for commerce. For them, business was not a noble profession. They believed in good social order as the incentive for pursuing the common good. Smith didn't consider business noble either, but he viewed it as respectable. A market economy is moral, he believed, because it raises the standard of living for all. Although motivated by self–interest, the net result of this new type of capitalism was that quality products were produced in abundance and at a reasonable cost. Smith assumed that such economic self–interest would be kept in check by the moral forces within the community. Regrettably, Smith's assumption did not always bear out. The means used by capitalists to stimulate economic growth often became an end in themselves. An economy based on the value of acquisition resulted in an acquisitive society.

THE GROWTH OF CAPITALISM

By the early 1800s, the French Revolution and the Napoleonic Wars had swept the remnants of feudalism into oblivion. The American Revolution had established new ideas about democracy and equality. Adam Smith's economic concepts were increasingly put into practice. Norms of economic life became free trade (demanded by merchants and industrialists), sound money (the gold standard insisted upon by bankers), and minimum levels of relief for the poor (thus keeping a ready supply of eager labor willing to work at low wages).

In practice, it was discovered that capitalism caused cycles. Agricultural farming gave way to sheep raising, for example, because wool was in greater demand and more profitable than produce. Farm workers then drifted into the cities because there was no work on the farms. A surplus of labor was then created; wages and prices dropped; women and children were forced to work (and were abused on the job). Finally, monopolies were developed that controlled and lowered the price of the raw wool that had begun the cycle in the first place. The effect of capitalism was to create a new class of nonroyal wealthy and nonrural poor that only a Charles Dickens could accurately chronicle.

World War I marked a turning point in the development of capitalism. International markets shrank; the gold standard was abandoned in favor of managed national currencies; the dominance of banks passed from Europe to the United States; African and Asian people began successful revolts against European colonialism; trade barriers multiplied; unions gained power; rules clarifying what was permissible in pricing, wage setting, and employee practices were developed. The Great Depression of the 1930s brought the policy of *laissez–faire* into question. After World War II, however, a free–market economy began to flourish again, especially in the United States and the defeated nations, Germany and Japan.

CHURCH RESPONSE

British economist John Maynard Keynes (1883–1946) may have echoed the sentiments of the church when he observed that "capitalism, wisely managed, can probably be made more efficient for attaining greater economic ends than any alternative system yet in sight." But he warned that capitalism "in itself is in many ways extremely objectionable."

The church has never condemned capitalism as such. Yet once the term came into general use, the church lost no time in issuing guidelines for its implementation. Benchmark church documents that include a commentary on capitalism — often termed the great "social encyclicals" — began in 1891 with Leo XIII's *Rerum Novarum*, the anniversaries of which were marked by Pius XI's *Quadragesimo Anno* in 1931, Paul VI's *Octogesima Adveniens* in 1971 and Pope John Paul's *Centesimus Annus* in 1991.

Leo taught that the unregulated pursuit of economic gain could lead to a situation where human beings are regarded as a mere commodity and that, while private property is a natural right, it must not be used without consideration of the welfare of others. "Concentrated economic power is as much a threat to individual liberty as concentrated political power," he cautioned.

Pius XI called attention to the fact that Leo XIII's whole endeavor was to adjust the economic regime to the standards of true order. "Surely, " he added, "the system is not vicious by its very nature." Nonetheless, he used words such as "direct," "watch," "urge," and "restrain" when speaking of the role of the state in putting reasonable limits on the excesses of capitalism. He referred to the theory of uncontrolled competition as a "poisoned spring" from which have emerged all the errors of individualism. He wrote, "It is just that any man who does a service to society and increases the general wealth should himself have a due share of the increased public riches, provided always that he respects the laws of God and the rights of his neighbor, and uses his property in accordance with the dictates of faith and right reason."

Quadragesimo Anno also set a principle that was destined to become the centerpiece of subsequent Catholic social thought: subsidiarity. This principle holds that it is a serious violation of social order to allow political entities to absorb functions that smaller and lower communities can carry out. The function of the state is to implement this principle with just enough force to ensure a real voice for all its citizens.

The point at which the state should inject itself into the private sector, however, has been the subject of wide interpretation. Unfortunately, the principle of subsidiarity has been used to defend some rather outrageous forms of capitalism. In recent years in the name of leaving decisions at a local level, for example, the White House has resisted the enforcement of environmental standards even when companies have violated them by as much as two thousand percent.

As early as 1940, Pius XI urged direct action. He called upon civil authority "to adjust ownership to meet the needs of the public good." Paul VI, in his 1967 encyclical *Populorum Progressio*, also urged that, when necessary, the state translate the "common good" principle into action. "The common good at times demands the expropriation of an estate if it happens that some estates impede the common prosperity," he wrote. Later, in *Octogesima Adveniens*, he cautioned that the state must "be able to stand aside from the particular interests of power elites and act on behalf of the common good." Paul believed that many of the hardships we now face trace their origins to some form of capitalism.

But if Paul VI was outspoken, John Paul II sounded as angry as Jesus did with the moneychangers in the temple.

In 1980, in his encyclical *Laborem Exercens*, he harshly criticized any economic system, capitalist or collectivist, that reduces humanity to a mere instrument. Earlier popes had called for a balance between capital and labor. John Paul's comments imply a priority of labor over capital.

In *Laborem Exercens*, he advocated new forms of profit sharing, co–management, and co–ownership of productive property. During a visit to Canada in 1984, he shared grave reservations about growing concentrations of capital in ever larger corporations and expressed concern that free enterprise alone cannot guarantee adequate production and distribution of food. In *Solicitudo Rei Socialis* (1988), John Paul II made apologists for unexamined capitalism pull back even further. His central emphasis was on the value of life at every stage and, in particular, of the worker and work itself. Like his predecessors John XXIII and Paul VI, the present pope never suggests the abandonment of capitalism; but he does point out that it should be significantly revamped if it is to meet the ideals of Christianity.

Perhaps the church's position on capitalism has been best summarized in John Paul's most recent encyclical on the matter, *Centesimus Annus*: "The church acknowledges the legitimate role of profit as an indication that a business is functioning well. When a firm makes a profit, this means that productive factors have been properly employed and corresponding human needs have been duly satisfied. But profitability is not the only indicator of a firm's position. It is possible for the financial accounts to be in order, and yet for the people—who make up the firm's most valuable asset—to be humiliated and their dignity offended. . . .In fact, the purpose of a business firm is not simply to make a profit, but it is to be found in its very existence as a community of persons who in various ways are endeavoring to satisfy their basic needs and who form a particular group at the service of the whole of society. . . .Profit is a regulator of the life of a business, but it is not the only one; other human and moral factors must also be considered which, in the long term, are at least equally important to the life of a business."

Maintaining the delicate balance needed on the issue of capitalism for Christians is not an easy task. Capitalism needs constant fine tuning in order to ensure that it is faithful to the biblical vision and the long tradition of the social teaching in the encyclicals and pastoral letters. The key words remain: common good, balance, and gospel values. Even business guru Peter Drucker in his basic text, *The Practice of Management*, reminds us, "It is management's public responsibility to make whatever is genuinely in the public good become the enterprise's own self–interest . . . (otherwise) the production of wealth will . . . weaken rather than strengthen society by creating social classes, class hatred and class warfare."

QUESTIONS FOR REFLECTION
AND GROUP DISCUSSION

1. Adam Smith proposed that if each person pursued his or her self–interest, the moral forces of the community would keep the economy in check. How would this work at, for example, a McDonald's franchise?

2. The U.S. bishops cautioned as early as 1919 that capitalism's full possibilities would not be recognized as long as workers were mere wage earners. Today some companies are being bought by their employees. Would you want to own part of the company you work for? Explain your answer.

3. Consider the *New York Times's* comment that there can be "no facile resolution of the conflict between the values of a just society and the sharply opposing values of a successful corporation" in relation to junk bonds and the debacle of the banks and S&Ls. How do these examples of capitalist excesses affect the ordinary person?

4. What problems have arisen as communist societies try to adopt a capitalist economy? Imagine yourself as a worker in a communist economy trying to change to a free market economy. What difficulties and dangers might you be facing?

5. Business guru Peter Drucker warned that, if management neglected the public good, "the production of wealth will . . . weaken rather than strengthen society by creating social classes, class hatred and class warfare." Cite examples of this in today's world events.

ACTIVITIES FOR FURTHER INVESTIGATION

1. From the daily papers clip five articles on problems of capitalism and five stories about capitalist successes. Discuss both aspects as a group or with family and friends.

2. For a week, read *The Wall Street Journal* or study copies of magazines such as *Forbes* and *Fortune* to catch the tempo of the world of finance.

3. Interview a manager about problems encountered in the labor–management arena. Then interview a union member or official to get his or her perspective.

4. Read the novel *Babbit* by Sinclair Lewis. Written in 1922, it portrays a prosperous real estate man who is a conniving social climber, an opportunist, and a conformist. Or try *The Bonfire of the Vanities* by Tom Wolfe, the story of the downfall of a self-styled "Master of the Universe" — a Wall Street bond trader. For a more positive view of a businessperson, watch the classic movie *It's a Wonderful Life* starring Jimmy Stewart — it's not so much a Christmas story as it is a parable about a capitalist with a heart.

5. Imagine yourself as a winner of a ten million dollar lottery prize. How would you invest it?

4

LABOR

In the early 1960s, the popular television show "The Many Loves of Doby Gillis" featured the main character Maynard G. Krebs, a beatnik who a few years later might have been called a hippie. He always wore the same ragged outfit, sported a scraggly goatee, and avoided work like the plague. "Work!" he would shout in a high–pitched voice at the mere suggestion that he should consider getting a job. While the reaction of Maynard G. Krebs was funny and exaggerated, his view of labor was not that different from that of many people.

Labor describes the effort involved in performing a productive task. It can also refer to a social group. Thus, the word labor has often been used to distinguish the working class from capitalists, the rich, management, or even the middle class.

The word labor has — unfortunately — some negative connotations. It often signifies toil, drudgery, even pain. The use of the word in connection with childbirth is no accident. Some still view labor as a punishment for the original sin. In Genesis 3:19, Yahweh tells Adam that as punishment for eating the forbidden fruit he and Eve will be banished from the garden and that "by the sweat of your face shall you get bread to eat, until you return to the ground from which you were taken."

The Judeo–Christian tradition, however, has also taught the dignity of work. Ecclesiastes (3:22) suggests that labor can have a positive side: "And I saw that there is nothing better for a man than to rejoice in his work; for this is his lot." Labor is seen not only as punishment for sin but also as a partnership with God in the process of creation. Thus, even today, the research scientist and the ditch digger are viewed as integral parts of the never-ending effort by humankind to use God-given gifts to improve the world.

THE CHURCH AND LABOR

Moses sounded like the first labor leader in his defense of the rights of workers: "You shall not defraud a poor and needy hired servant, whether he be one of your own countrymen or one of the aliens who live in your communities. You shall pay him each day's wages before sundown on the day itself, since he is poor and looks forward to them" (Dt 24:14–15). References to labor's rights are found throughout the New Testament. "The laborer deserves his wages," says Matthew (10:10) and Luke (10:7). Paul's second letter to Timothy insists, "The hardworking farmer ought to have the first share of the crop" (2:6).

Saint John Chrysostom, a fourth-century homilist, preached that labor was people's lot in life and that they could rest in the hereafter. Over the doors of Benedictine monasteries during the sixth century, signs appeared proclaiming *"laborare est orare"* or "to work is to pray." Saint Bernard (twelfth century) wrote that to labor was to lift one's heart with one's hands. And Thomas à Kempis (fifteenth century) asked, "Why should one seek rest when one is born to labor?" Saint Francis de Sales (seventeenth century) saw labor as a hedge against temptation: "Labor subdues the flesh like fasting. . . . In fact (it is) better to labor than to fast."

It was the theological vision of Saint Thomas Aquinas (thirteenth century), however, that shaped church teaching on labor for many years. Aquinas emphasized the duties of a responsible Christian in a highly structured social sphere. Those in charge would organize everything to the maximum benefit of all. As long as members of society fulfilled their roles, tranquility would be assured, since God reigned from the top of this hierarchically ordered universe. There was little room — or need — for individual or group rights of workers.

Sadly, a significant portion of the official church adhered for a long time to this Thomistic vision of society. (An encyclical barely one hundred and fifty years old, for example, said that any attempt by "the ignorant multitude" to change the social order was gravely sinful.) Because of this philosophy, the church made a very tardy entry into the struggle for labor rights. Little wonder that social critics of the Enlightenment, Marxism, and socialism were so hostile to religion.

The church has taught consistently, however, that human work is a continuance of God's creation and that society is a system of services in which all can take part. Labor, according to the church, involves the mastering of resources that God has created and that human beings discover. For the most part, the church applauds a technology which produces a measure of ease for people. It has condemned all societies in which the majority of members are poor and miserable; it has taught that those who labor should have a fair share themselves in the fruits of their work.

HISTORICAL PERSPECTIVES

The religious meaning attached to labor has been mostly positive, but in practice labor has had an uneven and tense history in relation to social status, capitalism, and just plain greed.

In ancient times, most labor was done by slaves. Slaves were initially the prizes of war and later an integral part of the economy. (Read Saint Paul's wonderful letter to his friend, Philemon, a Christian who kept slaves. It confirms the fact that slaves were so much a part of the economy that Philemon had a real problem with what to do when his runaway slave, Onesimus, became a Christian and returned to him. Nearly twenty centuries later, freedom lovers and slave owners such as George Washington and Thomas Jefferson had similar problems integrating their principles and practices.)

During feudal times, most farm labor was performed by serfs, who came to be regarded as the lowest rung on the social ladder. Social strictures held that "once a serf always a serf" — a condition that continued with modifications until well into the twentieth century in some countries. (In 1880, for example, Captain Charles Boycott, a ruthless land agent in Ireland, was ostracized by his serflike victims — thus giving us the term boycott.)

Medieval times saw the introduction of the guilds: economic and social associations of people engaged in the same business or craft. In time, especially in western Europe, the guilds set prices and standards of workmanship. By the late seventeenth century, however, the guilds' power began to wither. They were abolished by law in France in 1791 and by the nineteenth century had virtually disappeared from Europe (although they continued to operate in the United States until the founding of the labor movement).

Until the development of machinery, the refinement of the clock and the beginning of the Industrial Revolution, labor — while fraught with difficulty and danger — was approached more casually than it is today. The workday was from dawn to dusk — eight to fourteen hours — but was often shortened by weather conditions and the slower pace of life. Before society became secularized, religious holidays were frequent. The invention of the pendulum (1680) permitted time to be measured fairly accurately. Soon fixed working hours became the norm. During the Industrial Revolution, the working day expanded to as long as sixteen hours and the workweek to a full seven days.

Gradually workers became alienated from the fruits of their labor — and from their faith as well. Because the church depended on the existing power structures for its support and legitimacy, it often found itself on the side of "the system" in the growing disputes between workers and owners. By the time Karl Marx stepped into this controversy, the worker was quite willing to listen to his message and his ridicule of religion as the "opiate of the people."

LABOR UNIONS AND THE RESPONSE
OF THE CHURCH

The nineteenth century in the United States was great for the rich and terrible for the poor. During this period America's richest families were made, while workers suffered terrible hardships. Workers finally came into their own — but only after what amounted to a revolution that was fought one battle at a time.

The earliest labor unions were a product of and a reaction to the Industrial Revolution. They were started in early nineteenth century England and quickly spread to western Europe and the United States. The union movement came with pain and bloodshed. Employers and institutions fought unions as they would an invading army. Neither governments nor the church had particularly exemplary records of support for such movements. The church's reluctance to become involved in the cause of labor (combined with its sometimes vigorous support of the monarchy) caused losses in church membership among the working class in France, Germany, and Italy that have never been recovered.

When the church finally responded officially to the needs of labor in 1891 with the publication of Leo XIII's encyclical *Rerum Novarum*, it was already too late in some countries for the church to be viewed as a friend of labor. (Fortunately, the Catholic Church in the United States was a leader in support of the labor movement here.)

Leo XIII and Pope Pius XI are generally considered the giants of the church in forming the societal conscience on employee–employer relations. Their encyclicals are masterpieces — perhaps the most popular ever written. The path to *Rerum Novarum* began in Paris in 1868 when the future Cardinal Gapard Mermillod addressed an upper–class audience. He cited awful conditions under which workers labored, and he warned of the growing anger. He suggested that if action were not taken immediately to relieve their plight, workers would take action to change the established political order.

Mermillod and Count Franz Kuefstein of Austria helped to found the Fribourg Union in 1883. It was largely composed of laypeople who remained loyal to the church but understood that workers' problems could not be solved by discussions alone. For the first time, staunch supporters of the aristocracy and of the workers met and shared ideas. The union took a middle–of–the–road stance on most issues. Given the position of the worker a century before, however, even that stance appeared radical.

Father John T. Pawlikowski, in his book *Justice in the Marketplace*, writes of the church's awareness of "the need to respond to the deteriorating conditions that workers faced; failure to do so might lead to massive defections to socialism." The Fribourg Union guidelines became the basis for *Rerum Novarum*, according to Pawlikowski. They include: 1. No rejection of private property. 2. No support for class struggle. 3. No formal endorsement of capitalism. 4. A preferential option for the rights of workers. 5. Firm support of unionization.

The European documents had some influence in America. In time it became theologically acceptable for an individual worker or a union to make claims of rights against the state or the employer. It was a death blow to the rigid paternalistic concepts of Aquinas. The labor encyclicals, while late, may have spared the American laborer from the influence of Marxism. They certainly permitted a good many Catholics to stand up for the workers in the factories and the miners in the coal pits.

RECENT U.S. EXPERIENCE

The encyclicals may have helped save the American Catholic Church. The almost exclusively Protestant capitalist elite in America at the turn of the century had no relationship to the Catholic Church, while the laborer — often an immigrant from Europe — closely identified with Catholicism. Thus, the church was seen as supporting its constituency when it endorsed the rights of labor. *Rerum Novarum* stated unequivocally, "Labor . . . is not a mere chattel, since the human dignity of the working man must be recognized in it, and consequently it cannot be bought and sold like any piece of merchandise. . . . Labor is nothing to be ashamed of. . . . Justice demands that those who contribute to the welfare of the community should also share in it."

In recent years, many U.S. Catholics have moved up the economic ladder and become part of management and the middle class. As a result, some genuine tension has ensued over the issue of the church's identification with and support of labor and especially labor unions. It's likely, however, that without the union movement the condition of the laborer — even the one who never joins a union — would remain far short of the basic goals of dignity and economic justice for all.

In 1882, the first Labor Day was celebrated in New York. In 1913, the U.S. Department of Labor was established to administer and enforce many of the gains made by the unions. But the union movement — and labor in general — has hit a slump in recent years. When President Reagan fired over eleven thousand striking air-traffic controllers in 1981, he destroyed their union in a single stroke and sent a clear signal to employers that changed the whole tenor of labor relations in America. Today, more and more companies employ union-busting tactics such as hiring replacement workers during strikes or declaring bankruptcy in order to unilaterally void union contracts.

THE CHURCH AND ITS OWN WORKERS

Pope John Paul II's 1981 letter *Laborem Exercens* is more specific than *Rerum Novarum* and *Quadragesimo Anno* on the rights of labor. The encyclical covers a range of issues, including the links of labor with the economy, the role of women, working mothers, disabled persons, health care, foreign workers, new technologies, exploitation by multinational corporations, and a family wage. "Through work,"

John Paul says, "man must earn his daily bread and contribute to the continual advance of science and technology and, above all, to elevating increasingly the cultural and moral level of the society within which he lives in community with those who belong to the same family."

The American Catholic Church has supported labor — outside church walls. Its record inside, however, does not hold up as well. Its treatment of religious sisters may be a classic example. Sisters received food, shelter, clothing, and stipends as low as thirty dollars per month, with no provision for pensions or Social Security. Their assumption was that they would be cared for by their order in their old age. With the decline in the number of younger sisters and the changes in the economy, however, thousands of elderly sisters now live far below the poverty line. An estimated fifteen hundred sisters are on public aid; others are barely existing. Some attempt is being made to provide restitution, but the effort has been meager and the results depressingly poor.

Lay employees in Catholic institutions have not fared much better. Teachers and hospital workers in particular have been notoriously underpaid. It is still not unusual to find Catholic schoolteachers receiving salaries so low that they are eligible for food stamps. Teachers' and hospital workers' attempts to organize unions have met severe and repressive opposition in several major dioceses. Some bishops have even permitted Catholic institutions to hire union–busting firms.

In an article he wrote for *America* magazine ("Putting Our Own House in Order"), Bishop William F. McManus, retired bishop of Fort Wayne–South Bend, Indiana, challenged fellow bishops to practice what they preached inside their own institutions. Most responded to his call for self-examination with silence, others with criticism. The church simply could not afford such reforms, opponents said. Father Andrew Greeley commented, "It was the same excuse that everyone else has used for paying substandard wages."

In 1986, the American bishops issued their pastoral on the economy, *Economic Justice for All: Catholic Social Teaching and the U.S. Economy*. Initially the bishops omitted any reference to the "practice what you preach" question. Eventually, however, many of them insisted that the church address its own obligations. Thus Chapter Five of the letter states:

> We bishops commit ourselves to the principle that those who serve the church — laity, clergy, and religious — should receive a sufficient livelihood and the social benefits provided by responsible employers of our nation. . . . All Church institutions must also fully recognize the rights of employees to organize and bargain collectively with the institution through whatsoever association they freely choose.

The first moral principle in the pastoral states, "Every economic decision and institution must be judged in light of whether it protects or undermines the dignity of the human person." Many say the church must apply this first principle to its own policies before its credibility can be assured.

QUESTIONS FOR REFLECTION
AND GROUP DISCUSSION

1. Teilhard de Chardin wrote of labor, "The effort of mankind, even in the realms inaccurately called profane, must, in the Christian life, assume the role of a holy and unifying operation." How does this attitude relate to your own daily work?

2. The invention of the clock changed the basic concept of a workday for both workers and employers. What role does measurement of time play in your work and your attitude toward it?

3. List the positives and negatives of your daily work. Share ideas about ways to cope with the problems and exploit the opportunities that fill the workday.

4. Women are finding places in every area of work today. Discuss examples of women who have made their way into the profession or occupation they chose. What makes the experience of women in the workplace particularly difficult today?

5. The "labor" of an avocation is most fulfilling. Share experiences of work you do in pursuit of a hobby, an art, or an intellectual interest.

ACTIVITIES FOR FURTHER INVESTIGATION

1. Read the help wanted ads in the newspaper and list all the words that describe the qualities employers demand (for example, aggressiveness, self–motivation, competitiveness, enthusiasm, etc.)

2. Watch a movie about a profession. Some good choices might be *Nine to Five* about secretaries, *Backdraft* about fire fighters, *Norma Rae* about factory workers, and *Stand and Deliver* about teachers. Make a list of the positives and negatives presented about each occupation.

3. The satisfaction of work well done is energizing. Talk with a carpenter, an artist, a writer, a shopkeeper, or other worker for whom work is a real fulfillment.

4. Talk with people who are retired. How has the change from a workday to more leisure affected them? Are they working in any way now?

5. The labor of housework is easily forgotten in the consideration of jobs. Invite a group of homemakers to share the joys and problems of their routine.

5

UNIONS

The song says "Look for the union label," but it isn't sung with the lustiness or conviction the American people once had about unions. A number of factors have conspired to weaken a movement that, within a single century, has transformed working conditions in the United States. These factors include foreign imports; the availability of cheap labor in developing countries; job growth in white–collar occupations not normally associated with unions (retail sales workers are up thirty–four percent since 1986, for example); improved technology; change in occupations (the average tenure in an occupation is now between six and seven years); corruption within some unions; enlightened (albeit anti–union) leadership in some corporations; and consistently anti–union policies by Republican administrations in office for over a decade.

In addition, management has relocated within the United States to areas not usually associated with unions — notably the South — in search of lower–paid workers. Many of these new workers are members of minorities who, partly from fear of reprisals, are not inclined to join or form unions. Furthermore, younger, better–educated people entering the work force are often unaware of the history of the unions that won the working conditions they now enjoy upon entrance.

The rapid shifts have caused people to forget that the American union movement may be second only to the civil rights movement in its record of seeking justice for what is still considered one of the finest work forces in the world. No other societal group has done more for the working person than the unions. Churches, universities, social agencies, state and federal governments must all take a distant second place. The union member, together with the owner of the small business and the middle–management employee, still makes up the bulk of America's middle class. While unions and union influence have been reduced of late (in 1988 they represented less than seventeen percent of the work force), the work rules and benefit packages they fought for remain firmly in place.

None of these gains were achieved without bitter struggles, often marked by bloodshed and death. Generally, the pattern was the same: poor working conditions, organization of a union, failed negotiations, strikes, government supporting management by supplying police or troops to drive strikers from the gates, and finally renewed negotiations and settlement.

THE EARLY CONDITION OF U.S. WORKERS

The brilliant and perceptive French visitor to the infant United States, Alexis de Tocqueville, was only in his twenties when he published his classic study *Democracy in America*. His concerns for justice dominated his life, and he was fascinated by what he observed to be "the general equality of condition among the people" in this country. The fact is, however, early America had very little equality of condition.

In the early nineteenth century in Philadelphia — about the time of De Tocqueville's visit — working–class families often lived in tenements, usually one room per family.

The near absence of city sewers caused epidemics in 1832, 1837, and 1842 — all before the major immigrations that began in the late 1840s put even greater pressure on city housing and public services. As is still happening in this country today, the rich fled the city while the poor stayed behind.

Howard Zinn, in his book *A People's History of the United States*, writes that the consciousness of the working class tends to be fragmented and lost in history. Indeed, for nearly the first hundred years following the signing of the Constitution, little heed was paid to the plight of the industrial worker. Social historian J. C. Furnas comments that lager beer — imported with the immigrant Germans — swept the country faster than the labor movement!

Zinn cites an "unlettered mechanic," probably a shoemaker, who wrote, "We find ourselves oppressed on every hand — we labor hard to produce all the comforts of life for others, while we ourselves obtain but a scanty portion, and even that in the present state of society depends on the will of the employers."

In 1837 in New York, two hundred thousand out of a population of half a million were living, as one observer put it, "in utter and hopeless distress." Class distinctions were carefully drawn. The "ruff scuff" simply did not associate with those who carried gold-headed canes. Southern politicians boasted that the lot of the slave was more stable than that of the working class in the North. It would be decades before Marx's doctrine of class struggle reached American shores, by which time his philosophy would be tied to communism and condemned. Clearly, however, workers in early America had little to lose but their chains.

HISTORY OF UNIONS

In present–day parlance, there are two chief types of unions. One is the horizontal or craft union, in which all the members are skilled in a certain craft. Such unions could be said to have roots in the feudal guilds and were known in major cities in the United States as early as the late 1700s. The other type of union is the vertical or industrial union, composed of workers in the same industry, whatever their specialty or trade (for example, the United Automobile Workers of America). Industrial unions were organized in this country only in the last seventy–five years.

Although there were associations of journeymen under the guild system, trade unions had their real beginnings with the Industrial Revolution. In England, after the French Revolution, fear of uprisings by the working classes led to repressive laws against "industrial combinations." The repeal of these laws in 1824 resulted in a rapid growth in unions. In the late 1800s, the socialist movement began to make headway into the unions. In Europe to the present day, most unions are identified with rival Christian and socialist trade–union movements. Even Russia had a strong trade–union movement, one that backed the Communist movement that took power in the 1917 revolution. After the revolution, the unions were used merely as an instrument of the state in the drive for higher production and for communist propaganda.

Elsewhere, notably in Asia and Africa, the union movement in many countries became a strong force in the overthrow of colonial governments and the move toward political independence. The World Federation of Trade Unions and the International Confederation of Free Trade Unions were both formed in 1949. The former was largely communist controlled and boasted ninety–two million members in 1957; the latter was based in the Western democracies and claimed fifty–seven million members in 1960. Both have had significant influence on the education and training of people in underdeveloped countries.

THE RISE OF UNIONS IN THE UNITED STATES

In the United States, unionism in some form is almost as old as the nation itself. Skilled immigrants were drawn to unions, just as they had been to trade groups in their native countries. There were associations of journeymen in colonial America, but the Federal Society of Journeymen Cordwainers (shoemakers or cobblers), founded in Philadelphia in 1794, is generally considered the first trade union in this country. Such societies were not unions as we might define them today. They were printers, carpenters, tailors, weavers, and others who formed craft unions with the express purpose of keeping up the standards in their industries and preventing the hiring by employers of untrained workers and foreigners.

There was a measure of anti–Catholic sentiment in the early unions — a mixture of prejudice and anti–immigrant feeling that may have caused the Catholic clergy to be cautious about supporting the union movement. In 1844, for example, there were Protestant–Catholic riots outside Philadelphia involving Catholic and Protestant weavers over issues of religion and working conditions.

Initially, unions were formed in the highly skilled trades. Tailors, shoemakers, watchmakers, and the like could not be trained overnight and therefore could not be easily replaced if they went on strike. Gradually, the union concept began to take hold for all skilled workers in America.

Strikes were common and often marked by fighting and fires. It was the unions that fought for such "luxuries" as the ten hour workday and public education for the poor.

The upper class held unions in contempt. The typical attitude was expressed by former New York mayor Philip Hone, who called the striking New York City longshoremen "Malcontents . . . Irish and other foreigners, instigated by the mischievous counsels of trade unions and other combinations of discontented men."

It was still believed by many that the rich were the best judges of the needs of working people. An imported English common–law doctrine, once applicable in the United States (except Louisiana), held that in the absence of specific statutes, it was a crime of conspiracy for working people to organize for "militant" ends. The principle was applied frequently, and it served to take some of the steam out of the union movement until just after the Civil War.

THE KNIGHTS OF LABOR

In 1866, the first national labor organization, the National Labor Union, was formed. It had objectives such as the abolition of convict labor and the restriction of immigration. But when it attempted to enter politics in 1872, it collapsed under a volley of opposition.

The first real union, the Knights of Labor, formed in the 1830s but was quickly banished by sedition laws. They reorganized in Philadelphia in 1869 with a remarkable agenda: an eight hour day, no child labor, and no convict labor. Further, they welcomed female and black workers — an unthinkable concept at the time. In less than twenty years, the Knights of Labor had grown to over seven hundred thousand members. It used much of its energies in politics, however, and failed to focus on workplace issues. And with the rise of the American Federation of Labor (AFL) in the 1890s, the Knights dwindled in number and effectiveness.

THE AFL-CIO

The American Federation of Labor (AFL), was formed in 1886 out of a group known as the Federation of Organized Trade and Labor Unions, which had been founded in 1881. Both groups opposed the broad socialistic and political ideals of the Knights of Labor. Initially, the AFL sought only to be a loosely structured federation of skilled trade or craft unions. Members pledged loyalty only to their local group. Though the leaders of the AFL tried for years to avoid direct involvement in politics, they did succeed in influencing legislation that would secure shorter working hours, better wages, and the reduction of child labor.

When dissident elements within the AFL protested its conservative organization policies in regard to mass-production industries (such as automobile workers), they were expelled. The result was the formation of the Congress of Industrial Organizations (CIO) in 1936, which concentrated on organizing workers into huge industrial unions that represented all workers in a particular industry.

At its zenith, union membership, with over fourteen million members, accounted for some thirty-five percent of the labor force. Along the way, the unions won such important reforms as improved working conditions, safety in the workplace, the forty hour week, better wages, fringe benefits, profit sharing, pensions, seniority provisions, and many other rights.

THE DECLINE OF UNIONS IN THE UNITED STATES

The 1940s and 1950s were turbulent times for the unions. There were major mergers and breakups. John L. Lewis of the United Mine Workers helped to form the CIO, only to withdraw following a dispute with Philip Murray, his successor as CIO president. The garment–workers union withdrew from the CIO over Lewis's support of Wendell Willkie in the 1940 presidential election. The AFL had to grapple with the problem of racketeers and gangster–dominated affiliates; the CIO had a similar problem in ridding itself of communist influence.

Inevitably, unions became linked with electoral politics. The CIO's political–action committee, headed by Sidney Hillman of the Amalgamated Clothing Workers Union, played an active role in the CIO's attempt to enlist the support of its membership behind candidates whose election was considered important to labor interests. Gradually, the unions became virtually synonymous with the Democratic party, while management was linked with the Republican party. These political links continue. Candidates still seek the endorsement of unions, although such endorsements do not have the same impact they once did.

Labor's concern over the apparent anti–union policies of President Dwight D. Eisenhower (1890–1969) gave new impetus to the movement for labor unity. New leadership in both the AFL and the CIO made it possible for the unions to merge in 1955. The merger also gave them an opportunity to clean up their own ranks. In 1957, under the leadership of David Dubinsky, the AFL–CIO adopted an anti–racket code and expelled the International Brotherhood of Teamsters, the worst offender in extortion and collusion — with links to organized crime. (The Teamsters have since been reinstated.)

CONTRIBUTIONS OF UNIONS

Unions have been guilty as guilty as other institutions in our society of racism, sexism and operating on narrow self-interest. They have, however, also been among the leaders in promoting civil rights and social justice.

Throughout their history, unions have had to wrestle with De Tocqueville's image of the American Dream — work hard, obey your bosses, and you will enjoy unlimited opportunity. The image had ample support. Andrew Carnegie really had been a bobbin boy in a textile mill, and Isaac Singer — whose name stood out on the ironwork of his sewing machines — was once a wandering machinist. America was and remains filled with rags-to-riches stories, but the reality in this country is that only a few people make it entirely on their own and that most workers must organize to protect their rights and get ahead.

It would be difficult to gauge what social and working conditions would be like today if unions had never gained a foothold. One index, however, might be the current status of the many nonunion workers in this country (for example, migrant workers, hospital workers, and church employees.)

THE CHURCH AND UNIONS

Where was the church in the union struggle? The union movement sprinted ahead of a cautious institutional church. By the time the first social encyclical *Rerum Novarum* was released in 1891, the growth of social consciousness among Catholic thinkers in Europe had been underway for over twenty years.

By and large, U.S. church leaders were with the worker. As a consequence, the American church, unlike the European church, has not lost the allegiance of the worker.

Some clergy marched with workers during the many strikes that marked their struggle, and many Catholic laypeople took (and continue to take) leadership positions in the union movement.

Relatively recent church documents — for example, the 1933 statement of the American bishops titled *The Present Crisis* — state that "the tremendous increase in the output of industry during recent years . . . has not insured the worker the proportionate gain to which he is justly entitled. It has, however, vastly increased the incomes of industrialists and capitalists." Such sentiments fairly represent the feelings of the largely immigrant clergy toward their largely immigrant flocks.

QUESTIONS FOR REFLECTION
AND GROUP DISCUSSION

1. "My primary obligation is to return the greatest profit I can to my investors." What are the logical implications of this statement by the CEO of a company for such issues as product quality, fair practices, just wages, and potential takeovers?

2. What do you think of the push by unions for increases in the minimum wage?

3. De Tocqueville's image of the American Dream was "work hard, obey your bosses, and you will enjoy unlimited opportunity." Have these predictions of the "trickle down" theory held true?

4. The unions have created problems as well as solved them. What do you think about "right to work" laws that protect a worker from being barred from a job because he or she does not belong to a union? Unions have sometimes violently opposed nonunion workers. Do you consider this morally right? Explain your response.

5. The church has too often opposed the formation of unions for its own employees. The bishops, in their pastoral letter on the U.S. economy *Equal Justice for All*, affirmed the need for their own commitment to the principle of justice for laity, clergy, and religious in the employ of the church. What evidence of the implementation of this commitment do you see today?

ACTIVITIES FOR FURTHER INVESTIGATION

1. Some artists have spoken through painting and posters in support of unions. Ben Shahn (1898–1969), for example, designed many pro–union posters during the late 1930s. Find books about him and his work. (*Prints and Posters of Ben Shahn* by Kenneth W. Prescott has over a hundred of his graphic works reproduced.) Find a contemporary artist in your community producing artwork on similar themes.

2. Workers are often unaware of the role of the unions in gaining the benefits they now have. Invite a union veteran to share the tales of the early years of the unions.

3. If you were a union worker, how would you respond to a scab worker taking your job during a strike? Role–play the positions of both sides of this issue.

4. The unions have inspired many folks songs — Woody Guthrie's 1940 "Union Maid," for example. Find and sing the words to this and other famous union songs.

5. Investigate the policies of your parish, diocese, and other Catholic institutions regarding unions for their employees. Get involved in trying to ensure that those policies recognize the right of workers to organize and bargain collectively.

6

CHILD LABOR

Mary "Mother Jones" Harris (1830–1930), was working in a textile mill in Selma, Alabama, when the eleven year old daughter of a family she was boarding with died. The child's hair had got caught in some machinery and her scalp had been torn off. On Sunday, the day before the accident, the girl had been invited to a picnic but had refused to go, saying, "I'm just so tired I want to sleep forever."

Once a teacher in Memphis, Mary Harris married a man named Jones and went with him to Chicago, where she ran a dressmaking business until the Great Fire of 1871. It was at that time that she became involved in attempting to change the patterns of wealth, power, and poverty that had developed in this country. From 1870 to 1920, Mother Jones roamed throughout the land, agitating, organizing and preaching a gospel of justice and dignity for the workers. Her advice has become the battle cry of many social activists: "Pray for the dead, and fight like hell for the living!"

Mother Jones had a particular concern for children. She had lost her own four children in a yellow fever epidemic that swept Memphis in 1867. She had taken a job in the Alabama textile mills to see whether the gruesome tales of child labor were true. There she found six year olds who looked gaunt and aged working eight hour shifts for ten cents a day, and four year olds who had been brought in to help the older children without pay. In a factory in Tuscaloosa run entirely by child labor, she saw six and seven year old children crawl-

ing inside and under dangerous machinery, oiling and clean-
ing. Many times a tiny hand was crushed or finger snapped
off.

MOTHER JONES THE ORGANIZER

In 1903, Mother Jones moved on to Kensington, Pennsylvania, where textile workers — including ten thousand
children — were on strike. Maimed children had been wandering into the union headquarters, some with hands or
thumbs missing or fingers cut off at the knuckle. The vast
majority of these children were under fourteen; many were
under ten.

According to her obituary in the *New York Times*,
Mother Jones was a genius at organizing pageants of poverty and processions of the ill–used. She could vividly capsu-
lize social problems, the dimensions of which were so vast
they were generally ignored. With their parents' consent,
Jones gathered a group of seventy–five boys and girls to confront President Theodore Roosevelt (1858–1919) to demand
a law that would prohibit such exploitation of children. Each
child took a knife and fork, a tin cup and a plate in a knap-
sack. They carried banners and had a tiny fife and drum
corps. In a holiday mood, the children set out from Philadelphia, passed through New Jersey, and moved on to New York,
where Roosevelt was vacationing at his country estate.

Mass meetings on the horrors of child labor were held
in cities along the way. The group marched on New York
City, where the owner of an animal show put the children
in empty cages — a vivid visual image — while Mother Jones
spoke to the crowd. Finally, the ragtag army arrived at Oyster
Bay, Roosevelt's home. The president of the United States
(one of the four memorialized on Mount Rushmore) refused
to see them!

Meanwhile, the strike back in Kensington had been lost, and the children were forced to return to work. But not for long. Newly aroused public opinion led the Pennsylvania legislature to pass a new child labor law. Children by the thousands were set free from the mills, and additional thousands were kept out of the factories, at least until they were fourteen.

CULTURAL PERSPECTIVES

The point separating childhood and adulthood varies from culture to culture. For most cultures, however, a good rule of thumb is that childhood ends when the child begins to contribute economically to the family by full time work or leaves the family entirely to live an independent life.

The majority of the world's population is, and always has been, desperately poor. Children of the poor are usually forced to become productive members of the community at a very early age. In a study called *The Family in Cross-Cultural Perspective*, William Stephens reports that nearly all societies put children to work before they turn ten. "Typically," he says, "work begins somewhere between the ages of three and six. The load of duties and responsibilities is gradually increased, and sometime between the ages of nine and fifteen, the child becomes — occupationally speaking — a fully functioning adult."

In the Western world, and from the very start in America, there has been a pragmatic attitude toward childhood. The family's chief concern with their offspring was to get them out into the world, to turn them from economic liabilities to economic assets. At about seven years old, children were thrown into adult life. The poor went to work in the fields; others were bound as apprentices to local craftsmen or to serve in rich peoples' houses. Rich male children were taught the manly arts of fencing and riding as soon as they could walk, in preparation for their future career as military officers and gentlemen. Upper–class girls were expected to know how to run a house with a staff of servants by the time they were ten.

The very notion of a distinct and unique world of childhood, taken for granted today, was virtually unknown until the beginning of the twentieth century. It might be more accurate to describe the children of times past as little adults. There were few toys not shared by adults. Children's clothing was nothing more than a smaller version of adult dress. In most cases, children worked under the supervision of their own families, with duties proportionate to their age and circumstance. It was not until the Industrial Revolution that the labor of children was exploited away from the home and in hopelessly dangerous and unhealthy circumstances.

THE INDUSTRIAL REVOLUTION

Until the Industrial Revolution, the extended family was the basic societal unit, and the chief occupation was agriculture. Children helped their families in domestic and field work. The jobs were assigned on the basis of capability. Family dependency was a two–way street. Children depended on their families for care, but families relied on their children for economic assistance.

With the introduction of the factory system in the late eighteenth century, Great Britain became the first industrialized nation in the world. A run of good harvests had resulted in lower food prices; the plague had declined; health advances led to a lower death rate and a consequent rise in population. The growing population created a demand for more products and the increased consumption was a great incentive to industrial innovation. Soon, Britain was using more of everything — especially fuel — and its exports were growing even faster.

The need for more coal set the stage for children to go into the mines. Coal output increased over four hundred percent during the eighteenth century. Coal production led to coke, and the discovery by Abraham Darby of coke smelting in the 1730s revolutionized the production of cheap iron, thus introducing the first iron machines and structures. The development of inventions such as Kay's flying shuttle (1733), James Hargreaves's spinning jenny (1764), and Watt's steam engine (1769) gave birth to the industrial age.

Large quantities of cheap, compliant labor were needed for these tireless machines. While their fathers shoveled the coke that fueled the steam engine that drove the machines, the women and children ran the fast moving shuttles and the jennies. The system abused workers and destroyed them — especially young children. In 1815, Elizabeth Bentley, a mill hand, testified before the English Parliamentary Commissioners that she had started in the flax mills at age six, that she worked from 5:00 A.M. until 9:00 P.M., that she was on her feet the entire time, and that she was strapped if she was the last to complete her work. By thirteen, she was deformed; by twenty-three she was an old, pain-racked woman. Twelve hour days and six day weeks were the norm in the nineteenth century. When the abuses reached grisly proportions, the English Parliament finally passed a series of Factory Acts that restricted work hours and prohibited women and children from certain areas of work.

THE CHURCH AND CHILD LABOR

At first glance, it would appear that the church ignored the terrible problem of child labor. The more than two hundred encyclicals written from the seventeenth through the nineteenth centuries make virtually no mention of this abuse of children. (Even the sixteen documents of Vatican II do not address child labor directly.)

While the church was not unaware of the plight of children, it addressed the issue with its usual approach of presenting guidelines that are meant for all people of all ages. Thus, when the church condemned long hours of hard labor under poor conditions for paltry wages, it did so on behalf of all workers and did not single out children for special attention.

THE U.S. EXPERIENCE

The English factory system — working conditions and all — was imported to the United States. When the brilliant but cold-blooded secretary of the treasury Alexander Hamilton (1755–1804) submitted his plan "for the encouragement and promotion of such manufacturers as will tend to render the United States independent of other nations," he coolly calculated the potential of women and children working in the factories.

In the eastern and midwestern United States, child labor became a recognized problem only after the Civil War, and in the South only after 1910. Prior to that time, anti-child labor legislation was confined to a few states. Whereas in the past children had apprenticed to learn a trade or had worked in their family business, in the factory their employment — especially among orphans and indentured servants — soon constituted virtual slavery. In New England, young girls from large families were sent to the mills expecting to work for three or four years and then return to the farm where they would marry. But by 1826, a "mill girl" in Waltham, Massachusetts, was working in the factory for the rest of her life, earning two to four dollars a week — with a dollar and a quarter deducted for room and board. A writer from Tennessee, John Trotwood Moore, portrayed a cotton mill community in his long–forgotten novel, *The Bishop of Cottontown*: "Years in the factory had made them dead, listless, soulless and ambitionless creatures. To look into their faces was like looking into the cracked and muddy bottom of a stream which once ran . . . little, solemn, pigmy people, whom poverty had canned up and compressed into concentrated extracts of humanity . . . . They were more dead than alive when, at seven o'clock, the [whistle] blew and they left . . . a speechless, haggard, overworked procession."

REFORM OF CHILD LABOR

The first legal effort in the United States to curb child labor came in 1836 when Massachusetts ruled that children under fifteen could not do manufacturing work unless they attended school three months each year. Within the next decade, New England laws limited the workday to ten hours for children, but the laws were not enforced and even hard–pressed parents connived to fake the ages of their children. In the industrial towns, there was resistance to schools on the part of immigrant parents who still wanted to send their children into the factories, largely because the parents were paid so poorly that they could barely survive without added income from their children.

There were a few glimmerings of enlightenment. What historian James MacGregor Burns terms the "Common School Awakening" began in this country in the 1830s. The upper–class leaders of this movement wanted to provide a free elementary school education for all white children and to establish state control over schools. Gradually, more children were required to stay in school and thus avoid the abuses of child labor. Mechanization in the North, slavery in the South, and vastly increased immigration also combined to reduce the need for indentured servants and child apprentices. In addition, more and more workers wanted their children to get a better education, and labor leaders made free, equal, and state–supported schools one of their primary goals.

Implementation of reforms, however, was piecemeal. By 1852, Massachusetts had passed laws requiring children between the ages of six and ten to attend school for a few months of the year. By 1890, twenty weeks' attendance annually up to age fourteen was required. However, by 1900, four out of every ten nonagricultural jobs were still held by children, about seven hundred thousand of them. Children still worked in the coal mines. Although automated equipment existed, the owners preferred not to tie up capital in equipment when low–priced child labor was still available. In 1909, the *Handbook of the Women's Trade Union* was reporting that girls were still working in laundries — ironing one shirt per minute while standing for up to seventeen hours per day. According to Dr. Elizabeth Shapleigh, a physician in Lawrence, Massachusetts, at that time, a considerable number of children died within the first two or three years of beginning mill work, and thirty–six percent died before reaching the age of twenty–five.

National child labor laws were passed but declared unconstitutional by the Supreme Court in 1918 and 1922, although by 1915 thirty states required children to attend school until age sixteen. A constitutional amendment against child labor was passed by Congress in 1924 but was not approved by enough states. The Fair Labor Standards Act of 1938 set a basic sixteen year minimum age for employment of children producing goods for interstate or foreign commerce (with an exception allowing fourteen and fifteen year olds to work in occupations other than mining and manufacturing). It was President Franklin Delano Roosevelt (a distant relative of Teddy Roosevelt, who had refused to meet with the delegation of children organized by Mother Jones) who signed the bill into law. "A self–supporting and self–respecting democracy can plead no justification for child labor," he said. The Supreme Court sustained the constitutionality of this law, and child labor became illegal in this country. To this day, however, child labor is still tolerated in certain situations, such as migrant labor or undocumented immigrant sweatshops.

POST SCRIPT

Mother Jones was seventy–three years old when she led the procession of child workers to Teddy Roosevelt's home. As they marched, the children were carrying signs that read, "We want to go to school" and "A fifty–five hour work week or nothing!" While they didn't get to see the president, Mother Jones proclaimed, "Our march had done its work. We have drawn the attention of the nation to the crime of child labor."

When Djuna Barnes, a literary figure of the 1920s interviewed the aging Mother Jones, she asked her how she had started her career as a champion of the oppressed. Jones, then in her nineties, rose to her feet and shouted: "How does thunder and lightning have its start? . . . When a laborer sweats his sweat of blood and weeps his tears of blood, a remedy is thrust upon the world. I am the remedy. God has sent me to do this work and before it's done I can't die, and after it's done I can't die too soon."

QUESTIONS FOR REFLECTION
AND GROUP DISCUSSION

1. Trace the path of the child from farm to factory during the Industrial Revolution. Then compare it to the path of the young person to McDonald's and other fast–food "factories" of today.

2. Children in a farm environment share some responsibility for the work. Is there any comparable learning of responsibility in the lives of city children today? Is this kind of "child labor" desirable?

3. Young people today often work for school tuition or to share in the support of the family. Discuss the fairness of the minimum wage for these workers.

4. Education is essential today. Make lists of what you want from education or what you feel you have gained from it that impacts your work. Where would you be if you had never received any education?

5. What alternatives to a full college education are good options for young people today? What is the quality and availability of such alternatives in your community?

ACTIVITIES FOR FURTHER INVESTIGATION

1. Read one of Charles Dickens's novels about nineteenth century England to find vivid descriptions of the horrors of child labor (for example, *Nicholas Nickleby, Oliver Twist, David Copperfield*).

2. Talk with a teenage minimum wage earner about why he or she is working. Figure his or her salary against the expenses of taxes, transportation, clothing, grooming, etc. Decide if it is worth working for that amount to achieve those goals.

3. Learn more about Mother Jones and other reformers who fought against child labor. Investigate if there are any abuses of child labor in your community, then figure out a way to "fight like hell for the living."

4. Visit a museum and look at the portrayal of children in the art of the nineteenth century. Compare it with how children are portrayed in contemporary art.

5. The Children's Defense Fund (122 C Street NW, Washington, D.C. 20001) works for children in all areas of education, housing, health, and other issues and opportunities. Contact this organization to learn more about the problems facing children today.

7

WORKING CONDITIONS

Pope Leo XIII loved to write encyclicals. During his twenty four year pontificate, he issued nearly ninety of them — most dealing with social issues. While his other encyclicals are generally confined to the statement of broad principles, those dealing with working conditions tended to get very specific; for example, he called for a shorter workday for those "who quarry stone or mine iron, copper, and other underground materials." He also demanded some adjustment in working conditions for those whose work "is easy to endure in one season but cannot be endured in another."

This pattern of specificity on working conditions by a pope has continued until this day, growing more sophisticated with each encyclical. Thus, John Paul II's 1980 encyclical *Laborem Exercens* speaks of rest periods during the workday, holidays, vacations, pensions, and other benefits that improve the quality of life for the worker.

Working conditions have become a complex medley of rights and obligations, yet each change came about only because of long effort on the part of workers and their unions. It is a useful exercise, therefore, to follow the development of one reform in working conditions, and the fight for the eight hour day epitomizes the struggle for better working conditions. No other issue has caused so much turmoil in the workplace, and — with the possible exception of the hourly wage — none has been so important in determining working conditions for the vast majority of workers.

THE EIGHT HOUR DAY

Nobel Prize–winning novelist William Faulkner has observed that people are not asked to do anything for eight or more hours per day except work (and perhaps sleep, but that is another matter). Even in the most family centered homes, work takes a time precedence over other priorities. The eight hour day not only affects the economy, but it dictates the quality of family and community life as we know it. In many ways, the eight hour day remains the weather vane of working conditions.

The eight hour day and the forty hour week are now integral parts of the American work ethic. Like the seniority system and the division of labor, they form one of the cornerstones of labor agreements. Indeed, when the economy stumbles, union leaders will tolerate layoffs of junior workers rather than negotiate a shorter workday. (Senior workers are more loyal to their unions than junior workers precisely for this reason.)

In medieval times, productivity—in the sense of output per unit of time—was unknown. People worked from dawn to dusk, but the pace was more casual and work holidays abounded. With the technical development of accurate clocks, however, time gradually began to dictate the workday. Then came the Industrial Revolution with its factory whistle, time clocks, and output quotas.

Prior to 1886 in this country, most laborers worked a ten hour day, six days a week. Most transportation workers put in at least eighty hours per week, and New York City bakers worked up to one hundred and twenty hours per week. Their lives were not unlike workers in medieval times when the young apprentice was required "to sleep on one ear" in order to wake up at any time his master called.

THE FIGHT FOR THE EIGHT HOUR DAY

The movement toward the eight hour day has a relatively brief but violent history. In New Hampshire in 1847, legislation established that the ten hour day was to be considered a day's work unless an employee agreed otherwise. (Thus, even this law was ineffective because it could be — and was — bargained away.) In Ohio in 1852, a state law established that the amount of manual work for women and for children under eighteen years old should not exceed ten hours per day, but this law did not protect men. Furthermore, it was honored largely in the breach and was repealed in 1887.

The eight hour day was first advocated in 1860 by unions such as the machinists' and blacksmiths' unions. The first unified action toward the eight hour day took place on August 20, 1866, in Baltimore, Maryland, during the first congress of the National Labor Union. Seventy-seven delegates from thirteen states passed a resolution calling for the workday to be limited to eight hours. Industry promptly rejected this proposal as absurd and impossible.

Within a few years, however, laborers and mechanics who worked for the government contracts were given an eight hour day. In an act of Congress signed by President Andrew Johnson (1808–1875) on June 25, 1868, the government proclaimed that eight hours "shall constitute a day's work for all laborers, workmen, and mechanics who may be employed on behalf of the Government of the United States." The law was designed for internal use only, however, and had little impact on the private sector.

The ideas of the "union label," associated largely with the garment workers union, and the "union bug" still found on materials printed by union printers, got their start in San

Francisco in 1874 in the lumber industry. The label was introduced to combat the nonunion labor of Chinese coolies. A stamp pressed on lumber indicated that it had been milled by union carpenters who worked an eight hour day. The carpenters had founded the Eight Hour League in 1869.

ANDREW CARNEGIE

Although he was no friend of labor, steel magnate Andrew Carnegie was a pragmatist. When his workers informed him that being paid bimonthly rather than monthly was the equivalent to them of giving them a raise, he did so. When research showed that productivity actually decreased after eight hours, Carnegie also responded to his workers' appeal for an eight hour day. The morale boost did serve to increase production in Carnegie's factories. Other employers, however, stuck to the ten to twelve hour day, despite the example of Carnegie and the evidence that such long workdays were counterproductive.

Samuel Gompers, head of the newly formed Federation of Labor, made the eight hour day one of the union's objectives but, surprisingly, failed to muster the support from some of the other unions. Some of them actually sided with the powerful press who held that the eight hour day impinged upon the workers' right to work as long as they wanted. Other straitlaced moralists contended that if a man were given an eight hour day he would use the free time to carouse in saloons, away from family *and* job!

Some press lords assumed a middle–of–the–road position. Whitelaw Reid of the *New York Tribune* supported the eight hour day but felt that it would violate the right of workers to work additional hours for more money. (It would take until 1936 for the U.S. government to pass a bill that would actually pay workers time and a half for overtime.) For the most part, the notion that workers would receive the same salary for eight hours' work as they did for ten was simply too much for management to accept — even if it could be shown that workers produced as much in eight hours as they did in ten.

Historian Page Smith writes in his book *The Rise of Industrial America* that "the eight hour day aroused in middle–class and upper–class bosoms latent suspicion of, hostility toward, and even fear of the working class, a complex set of attitudes in which racial prejudices combined with a profound distaste for the freer, less inhibited life of workingmen, for their crudity and, above all their differences."

THE CHURCH AND THE EIGHT HOUR DAY

Much of the opposition to the eight hour day stemmed from the quasi–religious attitude that work had a redemptive character. Even most laborers believed in the biblical dictum that "By the sweat of your face shall you get bread to eat . . ." (Gn 3:19). For many, physical labor was viewed as a path to salvation. Further, it was a measure of a man's (and a woman's and a even a child's) character. The movement toward an eight hour day was viewed by many as an assault upon eternal religious truths.

In the churches, those who inclined toward the doctrines of Christian socialism supported the eight hour day. The Catholic Church rarely gets into specific issues. Pope Leo XIII's great labor encyclical, *Rerum Novarum*, did not appear until 1891, and even then it did not specifically endorse the eight hour day. It is safe to say, however, that at the parish level the church's sympathies were with the laborer and the eight hour day.

THE HAYMARKET AFFAIR

There were prominent newspaper publishers and humanitarians who supported the eight hour day. President Grover Cleveland (1837–1908) endorsed the idea, and a number of members of Congress expressed similar views, especially Henry Dawes of Massachusetts. Their scattered efforts were largely ineffective, however. The movement did not become a national issue until Chicago's Haymarket Square riot turned working–class anger into deaths and hangings, political conflicts and philosophical debates that would last a century.

The Haymarket affair had its roots in a rather weak labor organization known as the Federation of Organized Trades and Labor Unions of the United States and Canada. In 1884, they resolved to make May 1, 1886, the target date for a strike to win the eight hour day. As the date approached, the federation itself had virtually faded away. However, the issue of the eight hour day and the strike called in support of it had developed a life of their own. In Chicago, one of the strongest labor towns in the country, the month of April that year witnessed huge rallies in support of the eight hour day, despite unanimous opposition from the Chicago press and all the business leaders. It had been a cold winter in Chicago. The bread lines were longer and the suppression of work stoppages by the police had aroused fear and hostility. Newspapers and conservative spokesmen denounced the eight hour movement as the work of anarchists and traitors. The *Illinois State Register* complained of "Communistic Germans, Bohemians and Poles, representing the lumberyards, coopers, bakers, cigar shops, breweries, and the International Workingmen's Association."

The campaign did enjoy some success before the May 1 deadline. Many employers around the country adopted a nine hour day and—in some cases—an eight hour day before the strike deadline. In Philadelphia, workers accepted a nine hour day rather than strike. Before the Haymarket horror, an estimated one hundred and fifty thousand workers across the country won reduced workdays.

On April 30, the eve of the strike target day, the railroad and gas company employees, the meat packers, the iron mill workers, and the plumbers in Chicago all went on strike. The next day, May 1, some thirty thousand workers joined in peaceful parades and demonstrations. May 2 was a Sunday and things were quiet, but the cauldron of unrest had begun to boil.

On Monday, May 3, there were additional strikes and rallies throughout the city. One gathering attracted six thousand strikers, including several hundred workers from the nearby McCormick Harvester factory, which had been run by scab replacement workers since February 16 of that year when its regular employees had been locked out in a dispute over unionization.

The main speaker at the rally was a popular revolutionary named August Spies, a man viewed as a socialist. In fact, the union had approved his appearance, but "socialist" was a buzzword in 1886, suggestive of anarchy, godlessness, and all manner of evil. Spies avoided even a hint of revolutionary propaganda and spoke mostly about shorter hours, urging workers to stand together or be defeated.

Minutes before his speech ended, the bell of the McCormick factory a few blocks away sounded. About five hundred members of the audience, most of them McCormick strikers, broke away and ran toward the factory. With stones and sticks the strikers drove the scabs that had taken their jobs back into the factory. The city had already supplied

McCormick with police to guard the factory. Soon two hundred additional police officers were called. Shooting broke out. When the battle ended, one striker was dead and six were seriously wounded. Six police officers were injured, although none had been shot.

By Tuesday morning, May 4, the media had termed the workers a "liquor–crazed mob." The mood was still ugly. There were more riots at the McCormick factory and by evening there were several demonstrations planned, the biggest of them at Haymarket Square. Only thirteen hundred actually showed up for the Haymarket Rally. August Spies spoke again, this time giving a twenty minute speech in which he blamed the "capitalistic press, the employers, and the police" for the previous day's events.

By 9:00 P.M., another speaker, Albert Parsons, mounted the speakers' wagon. He was a noted anarchist who had served in the Confederate army and had become alienated from his prominent Alabama family for marrying a Mexican. He, too, gave a mild speech, pointing out that the worker received only fifteen cents on every dollar the employer took in. He was followed by Sam Fielden, an English immigrant teamster, who had spoken for barely ten minutes when about two hundred police appeared at the edge of the crowd in tight formation.

Ordered to disperse, the crowd began doing so when a dynamite bomb flew through the air, exploding just in front of the police. Who threw the bomb has never been determined, but a terrible fight broke out between police and workers. By morning, seven policemen were dead and over seventy were nursing injuries. Civilian casualties were two dead and sixty injured.

The press went wild. It was open season on anarchists, socialists, aliens, and radicals. The *New York Times* blamed the workers; within days two hundred "troublemakers" had been arrested. Thirty–one people were indicted. Only nine were brought to trial, however, and two of these jumped bail and disappeared. (Once the trial got under way, Albert Parsons, one of the two who had jumped bail, walked into the courtroom to stand trial with his colleagues.)

There were no laborers among the twelve white males on the jury, only one of whom was foreign–born. The prosecution charged that there had been a conspiracy to riot on the part of the workers, although some of the defendants did not even know each other. All eight were found guilty; seven were sentenced to be hanged.

THE APPEAL

During the appeals process, the condemned men were given a chance to speak. They described themselves as martyrs for the union movement and the quest for an eight hour day. One defendant, Oscar Neebe, was a yeast peddler who saw that brewers were working fourteen to sixteen hour days. "They arrived at work at 4:00 A.M. and worked until 8:00 P.M.," he said. "My crime was to organize them. Hang me, too, for I think it is more honorable to die suddenly than to be killed by inches."

The appeals judge simply reaffirmed the earlier sentences (which were upheld by the higher courts, including the Supreme Court.) The prisoners' passionate oratory, however, had brought the issue of the eight hour day to the attention of a nation weary of unfair work rules. While the courts held their ground, the eighteen month appeal process allowed many people to think twice about the sentences and the issues. Rallies in support of the workers were held as far away as France and England.

By November 8, 1887, Governor Oglesby of Illinois received petitions from two hundred thousand people urging him to spare the lives of the anarchists. Oglesby met with union leaders such as Samuel Gompers, president of the American Federation of Labor. On November 10, one of the eight defendants, Louis Lingg, committed suicide. Later that same day, Governor Oglesby commuted the sentences of two others to life imprisonment, but the remaining four were hanged the next day.

Six years later, Governor John P. Altgeld freed the three defendants who were still in prison. He stated that they were innocent — as were the five in their graves. Altgeld was hung in effigy and viciously condemned by the press, but he refused to respond to the criticism of his actions.

REACTION AND RESULTS

The Haymarket Affair deepened prejudices toward "godless foreigners." It caused a serious attack on freedom of speech in every part of the country. It demoralized the labor movement and weakened the idea of industrywide unions for nearly a generation. However, it did focus the attention of the country on working conditions, particularly on the wearisome and lengthy workday.

From 1886 onward, the shorter workday became the major demand of trade unions in most countries. Until 1900, machinery was scarce relative to labor, but this began to change rapidly. Soon a car that took a week to produce could be made in a day. By 1920, resistance to the eight hour day on the part of owners and managers had diminished considerably.

Large businesses, such as the Ford Motor Company, began to introduce the "eight hour, five dollar" day. (The concept of a daily wage for an eight hour day would have an impact on how workers were paid until the hourly wage became common among most blue collar workers.) The eight hour day also laid the foundation for overtime policies, lunch hours, coffee breaks — even accumulated vacation time.

It was not until 1938, however, that the eight hour day, forty hour week was instituted as the norm by the Fair Labor Standards Acts. Workers continued — and continue today — to work longer hours, but at least today most are paid overtime or given compensatory time off for their effort.

Peter F. Drucker, a student of the economic landscape, has written that the eight hour day not only doubled human productivity, it also more than doubled earnings and gave the Western working world the greatest advance ever recorded in economic wealth. Once machines were subordinated to people, Drucker argues, both productivity and product improved. Technical advances, necessitated by the shorter workday, actually added years to workers' lives and thus contributed to their productivity.

Once management realized that morale and productivity actually increased with the shorter day, it experimented with other improvements in working conditions. Thus, the eight hour day marked the first step toward innovative work rules such as flex time, extended day care, shared work (two people doing one job), working at home, and a host of other innovations that are still being introduced.

A FOOTNOTE

At Chicago's Police Headquarters, there is a monument to the police officers who died in the Haymarket explosion. They were victims in the fight for the eight hour day. In an old German cemetery some miles away lie the bodies of the other victims of that battle, the workers who were executed unjustly for fighting for their rights. At their funeral, William Black, who had labored for the cause of the eight hour day, said, "We are here by the bodies of men who were sublime in their self–sacrifice and for whom the gibbet assumed the glory of the cross."

QUESTIONS FOR REFLECTION
AND GROUP DISCUSSION

1. We are the beneficiaries of more than a century of workers' struggles. Our work options extend to shared time, child care for workers, working at home, flexible schedules, etc. How do these options affect the productivity and spirit of today's workers?

2. Some workers are "workaholics" or "work addicts" who work many more than eight hours per day. Discuss the implications of this on the family, church, community and workplace.

3. What are your feelings about the right of workers to organize, demonstrate, and bargain collectively?

4. Today, office workers, teachers, and many others see "sick days" as rights and plan the use of them for private endeavors. Discuss the positive and negative effects of this development.

5. With the further development of technology and increased foreign competition, there may be less work for unskilled or uneducated workers in this country. How should this situation be handled (e.g., shorter work hours for everyone? guaranteed income for all regardless of work imput? paying people to pursue art or knowledge?)

ACTIVITIES FOR FURTHER INVESTIGATION

1. Talk to an office manager about his or her experience in managing employees using alternative work hours.

2. Read about conditions in Third World countries, where many American corporations are moving production in order to take advantage of cheap labor and unregulated working conditions. One good book to start with is *Cry of the People* by Penny Lernoux.

3. Today, a benefits package offered to a potential employee includes not only vacation time and sick days, but also insurance and retirement benefits. Try to obtain written statements of a few such plans and compare them. Which elements are most important to you?

4. Many office complexes today are so large that employees have no alternative but to lunch in the office dining room and stay in the confines of the building all day. Explore possibilities of exercise, spiritual growth, or cultural enrichment that could be (and in many places are) offered to employees within a workday.

5. Volunteer to work a twelve or fourteen hour day. Write a description of how you felt physically before, during, and after the day.

8

UNEMPLOYMENT

The melody of this jazz song is most likely buried in the sawdust floor of the old Chicago jazz club where it originated:

> Please, Mr. President,
> listen to what I've got to say.
> You can take away all of the alphabet,
> but please leave the WPA.
> Now I went to the polls and voted,
> and I know I voted the right way.
> So I'm asking, Mr President,
> don't take away that WPA.

The singer could have been a forestry trainee of the Civilian Conservation Corps (CCC) or a ditch digger for the Works Projects Administration (WPA). Their work was mostly physical and the pay was often only a dollar a day — but it was a job. It put money in one's fist. It gave a person a measure of dignity.

One of the most closely watched statistics in the United States is the unemployment rate. Technically, it is only an indirect measure of the people without jobs. It measures, as a proportion of the total labor force, those people without jobs who are actively seeking employment with the previous four weeks. It may rise, for example, when large numbers of students leave high school or college at the same time and begin to seek jobs, or it may actually go down during periods of prolonged recession when job seekers give up trying to find jobs and, in a sense, withdraw from the labor force.

The real rate of unemployment in specific communities, however, is significantly higher than statistics show. In cities with large African–American populations, for example, in is not unusual for upwards of eighty percent of the black males between sixteen and nineteen years old to be unemployed with no prospects of a job, although a much lower rate is always given in official statistics. Hispanics, the fastest–growing group in the U.S. labor force, continue to have a significantly higher unemployment rate than the general population, although this too seldom shows up in the general statistics. There is also developing in this country a permanent underclass of people without jobs who are never counted in the unemployment figures.

What to do about this social problem? The experience of the Great Depression and the "New Deal" of President Franklin Delano Roosevelt (1882–1945) may offer some answers.

THE CHALLENGE OF UNEMPLOYMENT

Not long after the initial experimental forerunner to the CCC and WPA got under way in 1933, President Franklin D. Roosevelt (FDR) sent his friend Frank Wilson to report on its progress. "I saw an old friend of mine," Wilson wrote to FDR. "He was digging ditches and laying sewer pipe. He was still wearing his business suit and street shoes because he could not afford overalls and rubber boots . . . but he showed me the coins in his pocket and said it was the first money he had in a year and a half."

The CCC and WPA provided jobs, not relief; foremen, not case workers; a chance to advance, not locked–in relief checks. "The Federal Government must and shall quit the business of relief," Roosevelt said in his State of the Union address to Congress in 1935. "Work must be found for able–bodied but destitute workers."

At the time Roosevelt said those words, there were over twenty million adults unemployed out of a total population of just over one hundred million. (Such a rate of unemployment today would mean that over fifty million adult Americans would be without jobs and looking for work!) These unemployed workers had already received support from the Federal Emergency Relief Administration — support that was commonly known as "relief" or "being on relief." In his speech, Roosevelt called for the creation of "a coordinated authority which will be charged with the orderly liquidation of our present relief activities and the substitution of a national chart for the giving of work." It was a call to action that would revitalize our country.

Two efforts of Roosevelt's New Deal — the CCC and the WPA — illustrate the problems of unemployment and government responses to it. These programs contain elements of solutions that could be useful today in addressing our nation's current unemployment dilemma.

THE SOLUTION

On the eve of Roosevelt's taking office in 1933, the United States had dropped into the bottom of the pit of the Great Depression. The banking system of the whole country had collapsed overnight; millions had lost virtually all their material possessions, and many had lost the will or the skill to find employment. For most, there was just no employment to be found. People's pride and self–respect was destroyed, and the health of many suffered from both physical and psychological causes. Newly elected President Roosevelt's ringing response to this national trauma was, "The only thing we have to fear is fear itself." He promised ". . . action, and action now." Roosevelt didn't cure every ill or right every wrong caused by the Depression, but he did, in the opinion of historian Milton Meltzer, "recognize that in time of crisis the federal government would take economic responsibility for its citizens."

During a White House breakfast on March 14, 1933, Secretary of Labor Frances Perkins, the first female member of a president's cabinet, described her plan for grants–in–aid to the states for work relief. It would be part of a bill being introduced in the Senate by Edward Costigan of Colorado, Robert E. Wagner of New York, and Robert LaFollette, Jr., of Wisconsin. Earlier, in 1931, Costigan and Wagner had introduced a bill requesting one billion dollars (an enormous sum in those days) to fund public works. It had passed the Congress but then President Herbert Hoover (1874–1964) vetoed it with a little sermon on self–reliance and the wickedness of government assistance.

Later, when Roosevelt's friend Raymond Moley delivered a more polished version of the proposal to him, FDR declared it "a stunning idea . . . putting an army of young men, recruited from the unemployed, to work in the forests and national parks." Roosevelt took an active hand in fine–tuning the project. He had supported a similar state program when he was governor of New York.

Roosevelt may have found the first seeds of such an idea when he was a student at Harvard under the famous William James. It was James who had first coined the phrase "the moral equivalent of war" in addressing issues involving justice. Roosevelt recognized that there were many people near starvation. His close friend and adviser, Harry Hopkins, would testify before a congressional committee that "People do not eat in the long run; they eat every day." Hopkins, a former social worker who would later head the WPA, told the politicians that "hunger was not debatable."

THE CCC

Within just a few weeks of FDR's inauguration, the Civilian Conservation Corps (CCC) was established. Membership was limited to young men, although FDR used his influence to see that some older World War I veterans were admitted. For a time, in fact, the enrollees wore ill-fitting World War I uniforms. It would be a year before their distinctive forest-green uniforms with the yellow patch were issued.

Membership in the CCC was voluntary. The structure was semi-military. Professional military officers—among them Douglas MacArthur and George Marshall, who would later become five-star generals and national icons themselves—organized the camps. Within weeks, the first camp was opened in Luray, Virginia. At its peak, in 1935, the CCC had over half a million workers in over twenty-six hundred camps nationwide.

Both Roosevelt and his wife Eleanor had a keen interest in the preservation of U.S. natural resources. He visited the first camp and promptly renamed it Camp William James after his college mentor. He found that the barracks were clean and comfortable and that the average cadet had gained fifteen pounds since joining the program. In time, judges dealing with minor offenses or petty theft began to offer the CCC to the offenders as an alternative to jail. Most accepted and, with decent food in their hungry bellies, were rehabilitated. At a time when all of the military services were rigidly segregated, the CCC enrolled blacks and other minorities. With the inexplicable exception of native Americans, the camps were completely integrated.

Under the supervision of experienced foresters, the CCC did reforestation, flood control, and soil conservation. They drained marsh lands, fought forest fires, and planted trees — more trees than had been planted in the entire history of the nation. They created many new state parks and recreational areas, adding immensely to the usefulness of the nation's natural wealth without destroying its ecology. The entire CCC program — over its nine year history — cost a total of six hundred million dollars (slightly higher than the cost of one Stealth bomber today).

There was opposition, of course, some of it from sources generally sympathetic to the downtrodden. American Federation of Labor President William Green said that the CCC smacked "of fascism, of Hitlerism, of a form of Sovietism." The Communist party declared that the CCC was nothing more than a "system of forced labor." Socialist Norman Thomas called the CCC forced labor, but young men were deserting the socialist ranks in droves to enroll in the program. Ordinary citizens loved the CCC. A Gallup poll, taken in the summer of 1936, showed that eighty–two percent favored its continuation. By 1938, seventy–eight percent of the people favored making the CCC a permanent agency of government.

Always operated by the War Department, the CCC was made part of the Federal Security Agency in 1939. But by that time, the winds of war were blowing across Europe and a greater emphasis was being placed on projects aiding national defense. The United States' entry into the war in 1941 meant that most of the enrollees in the CCC would be called to combat. Against FDR's wishes, Congress abolished the Civilian Conservation Corps in 1942.

THE WPA

Before the demise of the CCC, however, the Works Progress Administration (WPA) had joined the effort to get the nation back on its feet. Much more Depression aid had been needed than Roosevelt or anyone else had ever anticipated. Historian Page Smith observed that "what was needed was . . . relief in public works. . . . With work relief, at least, the government would get back a portion of its involvement."

In 1935, with a sweeping executive order, Roosevelt established the Works *Progress* Administration, later to be called the Works *Projects* Administration. It was an outgrowth of the Federal Emergency Relief Administration (FERA) and the Civil Works Administration (CWA). The FERA and CWA did not do contract work, such as sewers and bridges. These earlier agencies generally cleared wastelands and attempted to refurbish old neighborhoods. The WPA would do larger, more necessary tasks. Within nine weeks of its inception, it put four million people to work. Within six months and with a total budget of only three billion dollars, the WPA undertook projects all over the country for road repair, low–cost housing, public bathrooms, and projects aimed at getting electricity to rural areas.

The WPA virtually refurbished the country. It built over one hundred thousand buildings, including forty thousand schools that would put over fifty thousand teachers to work. There were seventy–eight thousand new bridges linking six hundred and fifty thousand miles of roads — all completed in under five years. Eight hundred airports were improved and hundreds of hospitals, city halls, courthouses, and health facilities were built in towns that until that time could only dream of such facilities.

Over an eight year period, the WPA employed a total of eight and a half million people for under twenty billion dollars (one–fifteenth the cost of the 1990 defense budget). The Lincoln Tunnel, Fort Knox, LaGuardia Airport, and Boulder (now Hoover) Dam are just a few of the WPA's better–known projects. Most of its efforts are still serving the country after half a century.

THE ARTS PROJECT

One of the WPA's most lasting contributions was to U.S. culture. In the early days of the WPA, Susannna Perkins, daughter of Labor Secretary Frances Perkins, remarked to her mother that the public buildings being built by the WPA were too gloomy. George Biddle, another FDR classmate, told the president of the need to support artists.

What followed were wonderful experiments in visual arts, writing, music, and theatrical productions. The WPA employed a vast corps of artists, scholars, writers, and students. In the first five months of the Public Works Art Project (PWAP), almost thirty–four thousand artists completed over fifteen thousand works of art, including four hundred murals and almost fourteen hundred other commissions. At the PWPA's height, musical performances averaged four thousand per month. The creative corps conducted eduction programs and supervised activities of the National Youth Administration. Among the talent employed by the PWPA were writers such as Saul Bellow and John Cheever; performers such as Orson Welles; and artists such as Ben Shahn, Raphael Soyer, and Robert Barrell. WPA artists helped lift Depression people out of their spiritual doldrums and provided a commentary and record of the effects of the Depression and the failures of the economic system.

RESULTS

The WPA had its critics. Some projects were seen as frivolous, even make–work. By 1940, however, while the WPA was employing three million, nine million more were still unemployed. Thirty percent of blacks, for example, remained on relief.

Inevitably, politics muddied the waters, with WPA contracts going to favored areas. A 1939 Senate committee report was sharply critical of the WPA, and a strike by thousands of WPA workers to prevent a wage cut did little to enhance the popularity of the agency. The outbreak of World War II brought drastic cuts in the WPA program, and by June of 1943 what was perhaps the most famous social welfare agency of U.S. history went out of business.

Looking back, historian Allan Nevins observes that "in the first three centuries, Americans have triumphantly mastered their physical environment." In the century to come, he says, they must learn "to master their social and economic environment." Both the CCC and the WPA were idealistic and visionary. Now, nearly fifty years after their demise, Americans still enjoy the forests and parks that were formed; travel the highways, cross the bridges, and drive through the tunnels that were built; use the post offices and schools that were erected; and read the literature, enjoy the art, attend the plays, and listen to the music that was created by the workers in these government programs.

President Roosevelt was willing to experiment, to try something new, in the face of the economic crisis he faced.

Perhaps his spirit has something to offer to us in our present economic situation. "A dole," Roosevelt said, is "a narcotic, a subtle destroyer of the human spirit. . . . I am not willing that the vitality of our people be further sapped by the giving of cash, of market baskets, of a few hours of weekly work cutting grass, raking leaves, or picking up papers in the public park." He then backed his oratory with action.

Under FDR, government for the first time recognized its responsibility for the economic well–being of ordinary citizens. Besides the CCC and WPA, other programs of Roosevelt's New Deal — such as Social Security and the Tennessee Valley Authority — provided lasting benefits for the country and its citizens. The New Deal put an end to the days of *laissez–faire* capitalism and moved the nation toward a healthier, more rational, and more judiciously sensitive economic structure.

THE CHURCH AND UNEMPLOYMENT

Unlike the Western European church, where the upper class was the mainstay of the church, the American Catholic Church has been overwhelmingly working and middle class. Thus, while the church in Europe tended to side with the power structure in labor and economic disputes, the American church was usually on the side of the worker.

A crucial figure in this development was Cardinal James Gibbons (1834–1921), the archbishop of Baltimore. Gibbons was a small, mild–mannered man, but he possessed a will of steel that refused to bend on justice issues. He became involved in numerous issues regarding the rights of labor. It was Gibbons who went to Rome and persuaded Leo XIII to abandon his plan to condemn the Knights of Labor as a secret society.

John Ireland (1838–1918), the archbishop of St. Paul, Minnesota, was even more forceful than Gibbons in supporting the working class. At a gathering of laity in 1899, he declared, "Laymen are not anointed in confirmation to the end that they must merely save their souls and pay their pew rent. . . . They must think, work, organize, read, speak act. . . . [and avoid] too much dependence upon priests."

Gibbons and Ireland were just two of the forward–thinking bishops in place as the Catholic Church in America developed from a missionary to an immigrant church, from an oppressed to a powerful force in U.S. society. No permanent, formal, central organization of American bishops existed until the formation in 1967 of the National Conference of Catholic Bishops (NCCB) and the United States Catholic Conference (USCC), but as early as 1919 the bishops began issuing joint statements that supported the eight hour day, equal pay for equal work for both sexes, prohibition of child labor, vocational education and other issues. Since the end of World War I, the bishops have issued a series of strong statements urging both public and private sectors to address the issue of unemployment.

In their 1986 pastoral letter *Economic Justice for All,* the U.S. bishops summarized their position on unemployment:

> Despite the large number of new jobs the U.S. economy has generated in the past decade, approximately eight million people seeking work in this country are unable to find it, and many more are so discouraged they have stopped looking. Over the past two decades the nation has come to tolerate an increasing level of unemployment. The six to seven percent rate deemed acceptable today would

have been intolerable twenty years ago. Among the unemployed are a disproportionate number of blacks, Hispanics, young people, and women who are the sole support of their families. Some cities and states have many more unemployed persons than others as a result of economic forces that have little to do with people's desire to work. Unemployment is a tragedy no matter whom it strikes, but the tragedy is compounded by the unequal and unfair way it is distributed in our society.

QUESTIONS FOR REFLECTION
OR GROUP DISCUSSION

1. Henry James called issues of ordinary justice "the moral equivalent of war." Comment on this statement in relation to the problems of homelessness, joblessness, and hunger today.

2. Consider Roosevelt's WPA and CCC programs from a Christian point of view. Consider these opinions:

• Franklin Roosevelt: "A dole is a narcotic, a subtle destroyer of the human spirit."

• Norman Thomas: The CCC is "forced labor."

3. Dream a bit. What could programs such as the CCC and the WPA do today for:

• conservation, recycling, pollution

• the homeless, the jobless, the hungry

• roads, parks, public facilities

4. Labor unions sometimes oppose programs that create jobs for the unemployed at pay lower than the going market rate. Why would unions be against such programs, and what might be done to overcome their objections?

5. Where is government money best spent? Discuss why and how.

ACTIVITIES FOR FURTHER INVESTIGATION

1. One fine product of the WPA writers' program was a State Guide for each of the then forty–eight states. Find an old copy of the guide for your state in a library. It lists every public resource, park, museum, city, and town in your state. Compare its report to your state's resources today.

2. Find WPA murals in public buildings in your city or town. Look in the public libraries, post offices, and schools. Compare these artworks to the public murals — and the graffiti — on the outside walls of buildings today.

3. Read or watch *The Grapes of Wrath* by John Steinbeck, written and made into a movie during the Depression and recently turned into a successful Broadway play. Also, read Milton Meltzer's *Violins & Shovels* and *Brother, Can You Spare a Dime?* for further information about the WPA Artists' Project and the Great Depression.

4. Volunteer to help in a soup kitchen or shelter for the homeless. Talk to some of the guests about their background. Determine if they would be interested in working in a CCC or WPA type project.

5. Interview some people who have been on welfare for many years and discover how they feel about it.

BACKGROUND OF KEY SOCIAL ENCYCLICALS

- *Rerum Novarum* by **Pope Leo XIII, May 15, 1891.**

  Literally "Of New Things," on capital and labor and the condition of the working class. This was the most significant of all the encyclicals before or since. *Rerum Novarum* broke down the barriers that separated the church from the worker. Never before had the church spoken on social matters in such an official and comprehensive fashion.

- *Quadragesimo Anno* by **Pope Pius XI, May 15, 1931.**

  Literally "In Forty Years," commemorating the fortieth anniversary of *Rerum Novarum*. This encyclical repeated many of the themes of *Rerum Novarum:* the dignity of labor, the rights of workers to organize, etc. *Quadragesimo Anno* also emphasized the immorality of keeping economic control in the hands of a few. It recognized the principle of *subsidiarity*, which held that higher levels of authority should act only when lower levels cannot deal with a problem.

- *Mater et Magistra* by **Pope John XXIII, May 15, 1961.**

  Literally "Mother and Teacher," on Christianity and social progress. This encyclical gave an updated interpretation of the classic theme of private property and introduced the notion of private initiative as an extension of private property. While *Rerum Novarum* and *Quadragesimo Anno* left responsibility for social justice with the individual, *Mater et Magistra* placed some in the hands of the state. (This encyclical needs to be read in conjunction with *Pacem in Terris*, literally "Peace on Earth," Pope John XXIII's other great encyclical.)

• *Populorum Progressio* by Pope Paul VI, March 26, 1967.

Literally "On the Progress of Peoples." A vigorous endorsement of *Mater et Magistra*, *Populorum Progressio* presented Catholicism as no longer tied to a social system based on natural law, but rather as a proponent of a pluralistic, decentralized approach to economic problems.

• *Octogesima Adveniens* by Pope Paul VI, May 14, 1971.

Literally "Coming upon Eighty Years," commemorating the eightieth anniversary of *Rerum Novarum*. *Octogesima Adveniens* cleared up any misunderstandings regarding the church's position on Marxism. While clearly not receptive to communist ideologies, it placed some limits on the notion of private property.

• *Laborem Excercens* by Pope John Paul II, September 14, 1981.

Literally "On Human Work." *Laborem Exercens* focused on the themes that work is central to the social question and that work has potential not only to dehumanize but also to be the means whereby the human person cooperates in God's ongoing creation.

- *Solicitudo Rei Socialis* by Pope John Paul II, December 30, 1987.

  Literally "On Social Concerns," commemorating the twentieth anniversary of *Populorum Progressio*. *Solicitudo Rei Socialis* presented an overview of modern social problems with some guidelines for action. It dealt with authentic human development and adopted a critical attitude toward both capitalism and communism. *Solicitudo Rei Socialis* warned that economic development alone may not set people free but only enslave them more.

- *Centesimus Annus* by Pope John Paul II, May 1, 1991.

  Literally "The Hundredth Year," commemorating the one hundreth anniversary of *Rerum Novarum*. *Centesimus Annus* brought *Rerum Novarum* up to date and tied it to "the preferential option for the poor." Done in the context of the collapse of communism in Eastern Europe and the Soviet Union, *Centesimus Annus* still criticized both capitalism and communism.

ACKNOWLEDGMENTS

As always, projects such as this are the work of many hands. Our thanks to the Chicago–based Claretian Publications, publishers of *Salt*, an award–winning magazine issued ten times each year for Christians who seek social justice. These essays appeared originally in *Salt*, beginning in 1988 under the general headings of "Upon This Rock" and "Salt Mines." Our thanks to Rev. J. Mark Brummel, CMF, editor; Tom McGrath, executive editor; and Mary Lynn Hendrickson, managing editor.

We would also like to thank ACTA Publications of Chicago, Illinois, who initiated this current project. Co–publishers Mary Buckley and Gregory Augustine Pierce and manuscript editor Rita Benz, BVM, have been enormously helpful in rechecking and rearranging the contents in such a way as to address the world of work and money in a somewhat coherent fashion.

The religious and laity and both Claretian Publications and ACTA Publications are Christians intent upon keeping centuries of Catholic social teaching alive, especially through their recognition of the Christian vocation in the world of work.

NOTES

NOTES

NOTES

NOTES

NOTES

NOTES

NOTES

NOTES

NOTES